Italian
Phrases
FOR
DUMMIES®

by Francesca Romana Onofri and Karen Antje Möller

Wiley Publishing, Inc.

Italian Phrases For Dummies®

Published by
Wiley Publishing, Inc.
111 River St.
Hoboken, NJ 07030-5774
www.wiley.com

Copyright © 2004 by Wiley Publishing, Inc., Indianapolis, Indiana

Published by Wiley Publishing, Inc., Indianapolis, Indiana

Published simultaneously in Canada

WILEY

About the Authors

After her university studies in linguistics and Spanish and English language and literature, **Francesca Romana Onofri** lived abroad for several years to better her understanding of the cultures and languages of different countries. In Spain and Ireland, she worked as an Italian and Spanish teacher, as well as a translator and interpreter at cultural events. In Germany, she was responsible for communication and special events at a museum of modern art, but even then she never gave up her passion for languages: She was an Italian coach and teacher at the Opera Studio of the Cologne Opera House and did translations — especially in the art field. Back in Italy, Francesca has edited several Italian books and works as a translator of art books, as well as a cultural events organizer and educator.

Karen Möller is currently studying Italian and English linguistics, literature, and culture. Before entering academia, Karen worked in the field of public relations and wrote articles for all kinds of fashion magazines and newspapers. She has had the occasion to work on German-Italian projects, including verb, vocabulary, and grammar handbooks and Italian exercise books.

Publisher's Acknowledgments

We're proud of this book; please send us your comments through our Dummies online registration form located at www.dummies.com/register/.

Some of the people who helped bring this book to market include the following:

Acquisitions, Editorial, and Media Development

Compilation Editor:
Pam Mourouzis

Senior Project Editor:
Alissa Schwipps

Acquisitions Editor:
Stacy Kennedy

Copy Editor: Kristin DeMint

Technical Editor:
Laura Barbolini

Editorial Manager:
Jennifer Ehrlich

Editorial Assistants:
Courtney Allen,
Melissa Bennett

Cartoon: Rich Tennant,
www.the5thwave.com

Composition

Project Coordinator:
Nancee Reeves

Layout and Graphics:
Heather Ryan,
Jacque Schneider,
Julie Trippetti

Proofreaders:
Susan Moritz,
Dwight Ramsey,
Robert Springer,
Brian H. Walls

Indexer: Steve Rath

Publishing and Editorial for Consumer Dummies

Diane Graves Steele, Vice President and Publisher, Consumer Dummies

Joyce Pepple, Acquisitions Director, Consumer Dummies

Kristin A. Cocks, Product Development Director, Consumer Dummies

Michael Spring, Vice President and Publisher, Travel

Brice Gosnell, Associate Publisher, Travel

Kelly Regan, Editorial Director, Travel

Publishing for Technology Dummies

Andy Cummings, Vice President and Publisher, Dummies Technology/General User

Composition Services

Gerry Fahey, Vice President of Production Services

Debbie Stailey, Director of Composition Services

Table of Contents

Introduction *1*

About This Book...1

Conventions Used in This Book 2

Foolish Assumptions 3

Icons Used in This Book..3

Where to Go from Here..4

Chapter 1: I Say It How? Speaking Italian 5

You Already Know Some Italian 6

Words that sound familiar...................................7

Popular expressions 8

Mouthing Off: Basic Pronunciation.......................10

The vowel "a"...10

The vowel "e"...11

The vowel "i"...11

The vowel "o"...11

The vowel "u"...11

Consonants that sound the same
in Italian as they do in English 11

The consonant "c"..12

The consonant "g"..13

The consonant "h" 14

The consonant "q" 14

The consonant "r" 14

The consonant "s"..15

The consonant "z"..15

Double consonants 15

Consonant clusters 16

Stressing Words Properly..16

Chapter 2: Grammar on a Diet: Just the Basics. 19

Setting Up Simple Sentences 19

Coping with Gendered Words
(Articles and Adjectives)..............................21

Definite feminine articles 21

Definite masculine articles...............................22

The indefinite feminine article 23

Indefinite masculine articles...........................23

Adjectives..23

Talking about Pronouns 25
Personal pronouns..25
Direct object pronouns...27
Indirect object pronouns..28
Saying "you": Formal and informal 30
Asking Questions 31
Introducing Regular and Irregular Verbs...................33
Regular verbs...33
Irregular verbs 36
Presenting the Simple Tenses:
Past, Present, and Future..38
Past tense 38
Present tense 42
Future tense 42

**Chapter 3: Numerical Gumbo:
Counting of All Kinds 45**

Counting Cardinals...45
Ordering Ordinals 49
Talking about Time 50
The four seasons 50
Decades 51
Months of the year..51
Days of the week..52
Times of day...53
Being early or late 54
Getting Addresses and Phone Numbers 55
Talking about streets 56
Describing your home 56
Using the verbs "vivere" and "abitare".....................57
Money, Money, Money...58
Going to the bank 59
Changing money...61

**Chapter 4: Making New Friends
and Enjoying Small Talk..................... 63**

Looking at Common Greetings and Good-byes.........63
Deciding whether to address someone
formally or informally...65
Responding to a greeting..65
Specifying your reuniting 66
Finding Out Whether Someone Speaks English 67
Begging Your Pardon?..69

Making Introductions....................................69
    Introducing yourself.............................70
    Introducing other people 71
Getting Acquainted 73
    Talking about where you come from 73
    Being you, being there: Using the verbs
        "essere" and "stare"........................78
    Talking about yourself and your family.............81
    Chatting about the weather 82

Chapter 5: Enjoying a Drink and a Snack (Or Meal) 85

Eating and Drinking, Italian Style 85
The Start and Finish of Dining Out 90
    Making reservations..............................90
    Paying for your meal.............................91
Having Breakfast 92
Eating Lunch and Dinner...........................93
    Savoring Italian soups and pasta dishes 94
    Using the verbs "prendere" and "volere"..........95
    Ordering from the menu..........................97
Savoring Dessert 99

Chapter 6: Shop 'til You Drop!................... 101

Departmentalizing Your Shopping...........102
Talking with a Sales Clerk.......................104
Sizing Up Italian Sizes 105
Choosing Colors and Fabrics....................106
Accessorizing..108
Stepping Out in Style...............................109
Shopping for Food....................................109
    Meats...110
    Seafood 110
    Produce..111
    Baked goods......................................113
Paying for Your Purchases 114

Chapter 7: Making Leisure a Top Priority......... 117

Acquiring Culture.....................................118
    Going to the movies 119
    Choosing your seat at the theater...............121
    Going to a concert...............................122
Inviting Fun 123

Getting Out and About 125
  Enjoying the wonders of nature 125
  Taking a tour 127
  Playing sports 128

Chapter 8: When You Gotta Work **133**

Talking Shop 133
  Common professions 134
  The human element 135
  Office equipment 136
Chatting on the Phone...137
  Calling from a public phone 138
  Calling for business or pleasure 139
Asking for People and Leaving a Message 141

Chapter 9: I Get Around: Transportation **145**

Getting through the Airport..145
  Checking in 146
  Waiting to board the plane....................................147
  Taking care of business after landing 148
  Going through customs 148
Renting a Car 149
Navigating Public Transportation..............................151
  Taking a taxi 151
  Getting around by train 152
  Going by bus or tram 153
Asking for Directions 154
  Asking for specific places.....................................155
  Getting oriented..156
  Asking how far something is 159
  Verbs on the move 159
  Locations you may be looking for 161

**Chapter 10: Finding a Place to Lay
Your Weary Head.**.. **163**

Reserving a Room 163
Checking in and Getting Settled 166
Using Plurals and Pronouns..170
  Making more in Italian 170
  Personalizing pronouns...173

Chapter 11: Dealing with Emergencies **177**

Dealing with Car Trouble 178
Talking to Doctors...180

I've Been Robbed! Knowing What to Do
  and Say When the Police Arrive...........................185
When You Need a Lawyer 187

Chapter 12: Ten Favorite Italian Expressions 189

Mamma mia! (My goodness!)................................189
Che bello! (How lovely!) 189
Uffa! (Aargh!)...189
Che ne so! (How should I know?) 189
Magari! (If only!) 189
Ti sta bene! (Serves you right!) 190
Non te la prendere! (Don't get so upset! /
  Don't think about it!) 190
Che macello! (What a mess!)................................190
Non mi va! (I don't feel like it!)............................190
Mi raccomando! (Please, I beg you!)..................190

**Chapter 13: Ten Phrases That Make You
  Sound Like a Local 191**

In bocca al lupo! (Good luck!)..............................191
Acqua in bocca! (Don't say a word!) 191
Salute! (Bless you!)...191
Macché! (Of course not! / Certainly not!)..........192
Neanche per sogno! (In your dreams!) 192
Peggio per te! (Too bad for you!)........................192
Piantala! (Stop it!)...192
Vacci piano! (Slow down! / Take it easy!)..........192
Gatta ci cova! (There's something
  fishy going on!)..193
Sono nel pallone! (I'm flustered!) 193

Index *195*

The 5th Wave

By Rich Tennant

"So far you've called a rickshaw, a unicyclist, and a Zamboni. I really wish you'd learn the Italian word for taxicab."

Introduction

. . . .

*A*s society becomes more and more international
in nature, knowing how to say at least a few
words in other languages becomes more and more
useful. Inexpensive airfares make travel abroad a
more realistic option. Global business environments
necessitate overseas travel. You may have friends and
neighbors who speak other languages, or you may
want to get in touch with your heritage by learning a
little bit of the language your ancestors spoke.
Whatever your reason for wanting to learn some
Italian, this book can help. We're not promising flu-
ency here, but if you need to greet someone, purchase a ticket, or order from a menu in Italian, look no
further than *Italian Phrases For Dummies*.

About This Book

This isn't a class that you have to drag yourself to
twice a week. You can use this book however you
want, whether your goal is to pick up some words and
phrases to help you get around when you visit Italy or
you just want to be able to say "Hello, how are you?"
to an Italian-speaking neighbor. Go through this book
at your own pace, reading as much or as little at a
time as your heart desires. You don't have to trudge
through the chapters in order, either; just read the
sections that interest you.

If you've never taken Italian before, you may want to
read Chapters 1 and 2 before you tackle the later ones.
These chapters give you the basics that you need to
know about the language, such as how to pronounce
the various sounds and form simple sentences.

Conventions Used in This Book

To make this book easy for you to navigate, we've set up a few conventions:

- ✔ Italian terms are set in **boldface** to make them stand out.

- ✔ Pronunciations, set in *italics,* follow the Italian terms.

- ✔ Verb conjugations (lists that show you the forms of a verb) are given in tables in this order: the "I" form, the "you" (informal, singular) form, the "you" (formal, singular) form, the "he/she/it" form, the "we" form, the "you" (formal/informal plural) forms, and the "they" form. Pronunciations follow in the second column, along with the English translations in the third column.

  In conjugation tables, we list the pronouns next to the verb forms simply to help you remember which form is which — in conversation, you don't say the pronoun (flip ahead to Chapter 2 for more on that subject).

- ✔ Memorizing key words and phrases is important in language learning, so we collect the important words in a chapter or section in a black box titled "Words to Know." Because Italian nouns have genders, which determine the article that the noun takes, how you form the plural, and so on, we indicate the gender with either [f] for feminine nouns or [m] for masculine nouns.

Next to the Italian words throughout this book, you find the pronunciations in parentheses. We separate syllables with a hyphen, like this: **casa** *(kah-zah)* (house). We also underline the stressed syllable, which means that you put the stress of the word on the underlined syllable. (See Chapter 1 for information about stresses.)

Because each language has its own ways of expressing ideas, the English translations that we provide for the Italian terms may not be exactly literal. We want you to know the gist of what's being said, not just the words that are being said. For example, the phrase **Mi dica** *(mee dee-kah)* can be translated literally as "Tell me," but the phrase really means "Can I help you?" This book gives the "Can I help you?" translation.

Foolish Assumptions

To write this book, we had to make some assumptions about who you are and what you want. These are the assumptions we made:

- ✔ You've had little or no exposure to the Italian language — or if you took Italian back in school, you remember very little of it.

- ✔ You're not looking for a book that'll make you fluent in Italian; you just want to know some words and phrases so that you can communicate basic information.

- ✔ You don't want to memorize long lists of vocabulary words or a bunch of boring grammar rules.

- ✔ You want to have fun and learn a little bit of Italian at the same time.

If these statements apply to you, you've found the right book!

Icons Used in This Book

You may be looking for particular information while reading this book. To make important points easier to find, we've placed the following icons in the margins throughout the book:

This icon highlights tips that can make picking up Italian words and phrases easier.

To ensure that you don't forget important stuff, this icon serves as a reminder, like a string tied around your finger.

Languages are full of quirks that may trip you up if you aren't prepared for them. This icon points to discussions of weird grammar rules.

If you're looking for information about the Italian culture, look for this icon. It draws your attention to interesting tidbits about Italy.

Where to Go from Here

Learning to speak a language is all about jumping in and giving it a try, no matter how bad your pronunciation is at first. So make the leap! Start at the beginning or turn to a chapter that interests you. Before long, you'll be able to respond **Sì!** when people ask, **Parla italiano?**

Chapter 1

I Say It How? Speaking Italian

. . . .

In This Chapter

▶ Taking note of the Italian you know

▶ Appreciating cognates

▶ Looking at popular expressions

▶ Starting out with basic Italian pronunciation

. . . .

*Y*ou probably know that Italian is a Romance language, which means that Italian, just like Spanish, French, and Portuguese, is a child of Latin. Latin was once the official language in a large part of Europe because the Romans ruled so much of the area. Before the Romans came, people spoke their own languages, and the mixture of these original tongues with Latin produced many of the languages and dialects that are still in use today.

If you know one of the Romance languages, you can often understand bits of another. Just as members of the same family can look similar but have totally different characters, so can languages. You find the same contradictions in the *dialects* (regional or local language differences) in Italy and in other countries.

If you visit Italy, you'll hear various accents and dialects as you travel the country. Despite the number of dialects, you may be surprised to discover that everybody understands your Italian and you understand theirs. (Italians don't normally speak in their dialect with foreigners.)

We don't want to go into detail about these regional and local differences here. Language is a means of communicating with people, and to speak to people from other countries, you have to find a way to understand them and make your meaning clear. Because using gestures to make yourself understood can be tiring, this chapter presents some helpful expressions to make life easier, at least as far as Italian is concerned.

You Already Know Some Italian

Italians love to talk. Not only do they enjoy communication, but they also love their language, because it's very melodious. Opera is famous for a reason!

Although Italians are very proud of their language, they've allowed a flood of English words to enter it. They talk, for example, about gadgets, jogging, and shock; they often use the word *okay;* and since computers marked their lives, they say **cliccare sul mouse** (*kleek-kah-reh sool mouse*) (to click the mouse). And Italians are like most others when they get TV remotes in their hands: Oftentimes, you find them **lo zapping** (*loh zap-ping*) (switching channels).

On the flip side, many Italian words are known in English-speaking countries, such as these famous food and beverage words:

- ✔ **pizza** (*peet-tsah*)
- ✔ **pasta** (*pah-stah*)
- ✔ **spaghetti** (*spah-geht-tee*)
- ✔ **tortellini** (*tohr-tehl-lee-nee*)
- ✔ **mozzarella** (*moht-tsah-rehl-lah*)
- ✔ **espresso** (*eh-sprehs-soh*)

> ✔ **cappuccino** *(kahp-poo-chee-noh)*
>
> ✔ **tiramisù** *(tee-rah-mee-soo)*

You may have heard words from areas other than the kitchen, such as the following:

> ✔ **amore** *(ah-moh-reh):* That word *love* that so many Italian songs tell about.
>
> ✔ **Avanti!** *(ah-vahn-tee):* You use this word when you want to say "Come in!" or "Come on!" or "Get a move on!"
>
> ✔ **bambino** *(bahm-bee-noh):* A male baby or child. The female equivalent is **bambina** *(bahm-bee-nah).*
>
> ✔ **Bravo!** *(brah-voh):* You can say this word of congratulations properly to only one man. To a woman, you must say **Brava!** *(brah-vah).* To a group of people, you say **Bravi!** *(brah-vee)* — unless the group consists only of women, in which case you say **Brave!** *(brah-veh).*
>
> ✔ **Ciao!** *(chah-oh):* Means "hello" and "goodbye."
>
> ✔ **Scusi.** *(skoo-zee):* This word stands for "excuse me" and "sorry." You address it to people you don't know and to those with whom you speak formally. You say **Scusa** *(skoo-zah)* to people you know and to children.

Words that sound familiar

In addition to the words that have crept into the language directly, Italian and English have many cognates. A *cognate* is a word in one language that has the same origin as a word in another and may sound similar. You can get an immediate picture of what cognates are from the following examples:

> ✔ **aeroporto** *(ah-eh-roh-pohr-toh)* (airport)
>
> ✔ **attenzione** *(aht-tehn-tsee-oh-neh)* (attention)

✓ **comunicazione** *(koh-moo-nee-kah-tsee-oh-neh)* (communication)

✓ **importante** *(eem-pohr-tahn-teh)* (important)

✓ **incredibile** *(een-kreh-dee-bee-leh)* (incredible, unbelievable)

You probably understand much more Italian than you think you do, because Italian and English are full of cognates. To demonstrate, read this little story with some Italian words in it. They're so similar to the English words that you can easily understand them.

It seems **impossibile** *(eem-pohs-see-bee-leh)* to him that he is now at the **aeroporto** *(ah-eh-roh-pohr-toh)* in Rome. He always wanted to come to this **città** *(cheet-tah)*. When he goes out on the street, he calls a **taxi** *(tah-ksee)*. He opens his bag to see if he has the **medicina** *(meh-dee-chee-nah)* that the **dottore** *(doht-toh-reh)* gave him. Going through this **terribile traffico** *(tehr-ree-bee-leh trahf-fee-koh)*, he passes a **cattedrale** *(kaht-teh-drah-leh)*, some **sculture** *(skool-too-reh)*, and many **palazzi** *(pah-laht-tsee)*. All this is very **impressionante** *(eem-prehs-see-oh-nahn-teh)*. He knows that this is going to be a **fantastico** *(fahn-tah-stee-koh)* journey.

Popular expressions

Every language has expressions that are used so often that they become routine. For example, when you give someone something and he says, "Thank you," you automatically reply, "You're welcome." When you familiarize yourself with these expressions and how to use them, you're on your way to becoming a confident speaker.

Table 1-1 shows you some of the most popular expressions in Italian.

Table 1-1	Popular Expressions	
Italian	*Pronunciation*	*Translation*
Accidenti!	ahch-chee-<u>dehn</u>-tee	Wow! (positive); Bummer!; What a drag!; Damn! (negative)
Andiamo!	ahn-dee-<u>ah</u>-moh	Let's go!
Che bello!	keh <u>behl</u>-loh	How nice!
Che c'è?	keh cheh	What's up?
D'accordo? D'accordo!	dahk-<u>kohr</u>-doh	Agreed? Agreed!; Okay? Okay!
Dai!	<u>dah</u>-ee	Come on!; Go on!; Hurry up!
E chi se ne importa?	eh kee seh neh eem-<u>pohr</u>-tah	Who cares?
È lo stesso.	eh loh <u>stehs</u>-soh	It's all the same; It doesn't matter.
Fantastico!	fahn-<u>tah</u>-stee-koh	Fantastic!
Non fa niente.	nohn fah nee-<u>ehn</u>-teh	It doesn't matter. (You use this phrase when someone apologizes to you for something.)
Non c'è di che.	nohn cheh dee keh	You're welcome.
Permesso?	pehr-<u>mehs</u>-soh	May I pass?; May I come in?
Stupendo!	stoo-<u>pehn</u>-doh	Wonderful!; Fabulous!
Va bene!	vah <u>beh</u>-neh	Okay!

Italians use the expression **Permesso?** every time they cross a threshold when entering a house or when passing through a crowd. A more familiar equivalent for "May I?" is **Posso?** (_pohs_-soh) (May I?; Can I?).

Mouthing Off: Basic Pronunciation

Italian provides many opportunities for your tongue to do acrobatics. In this section, we give you some basic pronunciation hints that are important both for surfing through this book and for good articulation when you speak Italian. (If you tried to read and pronounce Italian words in the English manner, Italian speakers would have problems understanding you, just as you may have trouble understanding Italians when they speak English.)

We'll start with the tough ones: vowels. Vowels are difficult because you have to cope with new sounds. Well, the sounds aren't that new, but the connection between the written letter and the actual pronunciation isn't the same as it is in English.

Italian has five written vowels: *a, e, i, o,* and *u.* The following sections tell you how to pronounce them.

The vowel "a"

When foreigners try to learn English, they are shocked to discover how many different sounds the English *a* can have. In Italian, the letter *a* has just one pronunciation: Think of the *a* sound in the English word **far.** The Italian *a* sounds just like that.

To prevent you from falling back to the other *a* sounds found in English, we transcribe the Italian *a* as *(ah),* as in **casa** (_kah_-zah) (house).

The vowel "e"

Forget all you know about the English *e.* Think of the sound in the French word **gourmet** (you don't pronounce the *t*). This sound comes very close to the Italian *e.* In this book, we transcribe the *e* sound as *(eh)*, as in **peso** *(peh-zoh)* (weight).

The vowel "i"

The Italian *i* is pronounced *(ee),* as in the English word **see.** Here are a couple of examples:

- ✔ **vita** *(vee-tah)* (life)
- ✔ **cinema** *(chee-neh-mah)* (cinema)

The vowel "o"

The Italian *o* is pronounced as in the English (from the Italian) **piano.** Therefore, we list the pronunciation as (oh), as in **dolce** *(dohl-cheh)* (sweet).

The vowel "u"

The Italian *u* sounds like the English *(oo),* as in **zoo.** Therefore, we use *(oo)* to transcribe the Italian *u.* Here are some sample words:

- ✔ **tu** *(too)* (you)
- ✔ **luna** *(loo-nah)* (moon)

Consonants that sound the same in Italian as they do in English

Italian has the same consonants that English does. You pronounce most of them the same way, but a few have noteworthy differences. We start with the easy ones and look at those that are pronounced identically:

- ✔ **b:** As in **bene** *(beh-neh)* (well)
- ✔ **d:** As in **dare** *(dah-reh)* (to give)

- ✔ **f:** As in **fare** *(<u>fah</u>-reh)* (to make)
- ✔ **l:** As in **ladro** *(<u>lah</u>-droh)* (thief)
- ✔ **m:** As in **madre** *(<u>mah</u>-dreh)* (mother)
- ✔ **n:** As in **no** *(noh)* (no)
- ✔ **p:** As in **padre** *(<u>pah</u>-dreh)* (father)
- ✔ **t:** As in **treno** *(<u>treh</u>-noh)* (train)
- ✔ **v:** As in **vino** *(<u>vee</u>-noh)* (wine)

Some consonants don't really exist in Italian, except in some foreign words that have entered the language:

- ✔ **j:** Exists mostly in foreign words such as **jogging, junior,** and **jeans.**
- ✔ **k:** The same as *j;* you find it in words like **okay, ketchup,** and **killer.**
- ✔ **w:** You find it in some foreign words (for the most part English words), like **whiskey, windsurf,** and **wafer.**
- ✔ **x:** As with *j, k,* and *w, x* doesn't really exist in Italian, with the difference that "x words" derive mostly from Greek. Examples include **xenofobia** *(kseh-noh-foh-<u>bee</u>-ah)* (xenophobia) and **xilofono** *(ksee-<u>loh</u>-foh-noh)* (xylophone).
- ✔ **y:** The letter *y* normally appears only in foreign words, like **yogurt, hobby,** and **yacht.**

The consonant "c"

The Italian *c* has various sounds depending on which letter follows it:

- ✔ When *c* is followed by *a, o, u,* or any consonant, you pronounce it as in the English word **cat.** We transcribe this pronunciation as *(k).* Examples include **colpa** *(<u>kohl</u>-pah)* (guilt) and **cuore** *(koo-<u>oh</u>-reh)* (heart).

✔ When *c* is followed by *e* or *i*, you pronounce it as you do the first and last sound in the English word **church;** therefore, we give you the pronunciation *(ch)*. Examples include **cibo** *(chee-boh)* (food) and **certo** *(chehr-toh)* (certainly).

✔ To obtain the "ch" sound before *a, o,* or *u,* you have to insert an *i.* This *i,* however, serves only to create the "ch" sound; you don't pronounce it. Examples include **ciao** *(chah-oh)* (hello; good-bye), **cioccolata** *(chok-koh-lah-tah)* (chocolate), and **ciuccio** *(choo-choh)* (baby's pacifier).

✔ To obtain the "k" sound before *e* and *i,* you must put an *h* between the *c* and the *e* or *i.* Examples include **che** *(keh)* (what), **chiesa** *(kee-eh-zah)* (church), and **chiave** *(kee-ah-veh)* (key).

This pronunciation scheme sounds terribly complicated, but it really isn't. Here we present it in another way:

casa	**co**lpa	**cu**ore	**che**	**chi**ave	= **k**
cena	**ci**bo	**ce**rto	**cio**ccolata	**cia**o	= **ch**

The consonant "g"

The Italian *g* behaves the same as the *c.* Therefore, we present it the same way:

✔ When *g* is followed by *a, o, u,* or any consonant, you pronounce it as you pronounce the *g* in the English word **good.** We transcribe this pronunciation as *(g).* Examples include **gamba** *(gahm-bah)* (leg), **gomma** *(gohm-mah)* (rubber), and **guerra** *(goo-eh-rah)* (war).

✔ When *g* is followed by *e* or *i,* you pronounce it as you do the first sound in the English word **job;** we write the pronunciation as *(j).* Examples include **gentile** *(jehn-tee-leh)* (kind) and **giorno** *(johr-noh)* (day).

✔ To obtain the "g" sound before *e* or *i*, you must put an *h* between the letter *g* and the *e* or *i*. Examples include **spaghetti** *(spah-geht-tee)* (spaghetti), **ghiaccio** *(gee-ahch-choh)* (ice), and **ghirlanda** *(geer-lahn-dah)* (wreath).

Here's another little pattern to help you remember these pronunciations:

gamba **go**mma **gue**rra **ghi**accio spa**ghe**tti = **g**

gentile **gio**rno **gia**cca **gio**co   **giu**dice   = **j**

The consonant "h"

The consonant *h* has only one function: to change the sound of *c* and *g* before the vowels *e* and *i,* as described earlier in this chapter. It also appears in foreign expressions such as **hostess, hit parade,** and **hobby** and in some forms of the verb **avere** *(ah-veh-reh)* (to have), but there it's always silent.

The consonant "q"

Q exists only in connection with *u* followed by another vowel; that is, you always find *qu.* The *q* is pronounced like *(k),* and *qu* is therefore pronounced *(koo).* Examples include **quattro** *(koo-aht-troh)* (four), **questo** *(koo-eh-stoh)* (this), and **quadro** *(koo-ah-droh)* (picture).

The consonant "r"

You don't pronounce the Italian *r* with your tongue in the back, as you do the English *r;* rather, you trill it at your *alveolar ridge,* which is the front part of your palate, right behind your front teeth. In the beginning, you may not find this pronunciation manageable, but practice makes perfect!

Here are some words to help you practice:

✔ **radio** (*rah-dee-oh*) (radio)

✔ **per favore** (*pehr fah-voh-reh*) (please)

✔ **rumore** (*ruh-moh-reh*) (noise)

The consonant "s"

S is sometimes pronounced as the English *s*, as in **so**. In this case, we give the pronunciation *(s)*. In other cases, you pronounce it like the English *z*, as in **zero**; in these cases, we list *(z)* as the pronunciation. Examples include **pasta** (*pah-stah*) (pasta), **solo** (*soh-loh*) (only), **chiesa** (*kee-eh-zah*) (church), and **gelosia** (*jeh-loh-zee-ah*) (jealousy).

The consonant "z"

A single *z* is pronounced *(dz)* — the sound is very similar to the English *z* in **zero**, with a *d* added at the beginning, as in **zio** (*dzee-oh*) (uncle). When the *z* is doubled, you pronounce it more sharply, like *(t-ts)*, as in **tazza** (*taht-tsah*) (cup; mug).

Double consonants

When you encounter double consonants in Italian, you have to pronounce each instance of the consonant or lengthen the sound. The difficult part is that you don't pause between the consonants.

Doubling the consonant usually changes the meaning of the word. So, to make sure that your Italian is understandable, emphasize doubled consonants well. To make you pronounce words with double consonants correctly, we write the first consonant at the end of one syllable and the second at the beginning of the following one, as in these examples:

✔ **nono** (*noh-noh*) (ninth)

✔ **nonno** (*nohn-noh*) (grandfather)

✔ **capello** *(kah-<u>pehl</u>-loh)* (hair)

✔ **cappello** *(kahp-<u>pehl</u>-loh)* (hat)

Don't worry too much about your pronunciation of double consonants, though, because in a conversation, the context helps people understand you.

Consonant clusters

Certain consonant clusters have special sounds in Italian:

✔ **gn** is pronounced as the English "ny." The sound is actually the same as in the Spanish word **señorita** *(seh-nyoh-<u>ree</u>-tah)* (miss).

✔ **sc** is pronounced as in the English **scooter** when it comes before **a, o, u,** or **h** — as in **scala** *(<u>skah</u>-lah)* (scale), **sconto** *(<u>skohn</u>-toh)* (discount), and **scuola** *(scoo-<u>oh</u>-lah)* (school). When it comes before **e** and **i,** you pronounce it like the **sh** in **cash.** Examples of this pronunciation include **scena** *(<u>sheh</u>-nah)* (scene), **scesa** *(<u>sheh</u>-sah)* (descent), and **scimmia** *(<u>sheem</u>-mee-ah)* (monkey).

Stressing Words Properly

Stress is the audible accent that you put on a syllable as you speak it. One syllable always gets more stress than all the others. In this book, we underline the syllables to stress.

Some words give you a hint as to where to stress them: They have an accent (`) or (´) above one of their letters. Here are some examples:

✔ **caffè** *(kahf-<u>feh</u>)* (coffee)

✔ **città** *(cheet-<u>tah</u>)* (city)

✔ **lunedì** *(loo-neh-<u>dee</u>)* (Monday)

✔ **perché** *(pehr-<u>keh</u>)* (why; because)

✔ **però** *(peh-roh)* (but)

✔ **università** *(oo-nee-vehr-see-tah)* (university)

✔ **virtù** *(veer-too)* (virtue)

In Italian, only vowels have accents. All vowels at the end of a word can have this accent (`` ` ``), but only the *e* can have both (`` ` ``) and (´). The difference lies only in the pronunciation. That is, *è* is pronounced very open, as in **hell,** whereas *é* is more closed, as in **gourmet.**

If a word doesn't feature an accent mark, you're on your own. A rough guideline is that Italian tends to stress the next-to-last syllable. But there are too many exceptions to list them all here!

Sometimes the inclusion of an accent changes a word's meaning. Fortunately, only a few words have the same spelling with only an accent to distinguish them, but the distinction can be very important. For example, *é* *(eh)* (and) and *è* *(eh)* (he/she/it is) are distinguished only by the accent on the vowel.

Chapter 2

Grammar on a Diet: Just the Basics

● ●

In This Chapter

▶ Introducing simple sentence construction

▶ Dealing with pronouns and gendered words

▶ Exploring regular and irregular verbs

▶ Working with different verb tenses

● ●

*E*very language has special speaking and writing patterns that make understanding easier. If everyone decided not to follow these rules, you'd have a hard time understanding even someone speaking your native tongue. Don't look at grammar as a burden, but more as a scaffolding that helps you to construct your sentences. Go ahead and roll up your sleeves; in this chapter, you find out how to lay the foundation with correct sentence structure.

Setting Up Simple Sentences

Becoming a fluent speaker of a foreign language takes a lot of work. Simply making yourself understood in a foreign language is much easier. Even if you know only a few words, you can usually communicate successfully in common situations, such as at a restaurant or a hotel.

Forming simple sentences in Italian is, well, simple. The basic sentence structure is subject-verb-object — the same as in English. In the following examples, you can see how this structure works:

- **Carla parla inglese.** (_kahr_-lah _pahr_-lah een-_gleh_-zeh) (Carla speaks English.)

- **Pietro ha una macchina.** (pee-_eh_-troh ah _oo_-nah _mahk_-kee-nah) (Pietro has a car.)

One major difference between English and Italian is that Italian doesn't usually put the subject before the verb when the subject is a personal pronoun, such as I, you, he, or she. This may sound odd, but the verb changes according to its subject. Consequently, if you know the different verb forms, you automatically understand who the subject is. The verb form tells you the unspoken subject, as in this example: **Ho una macchina** (oh _oo_-nah _mahk_-kee-nah) means "I have a car."

Table 2-1 shows the verb **avere** (ah-_veh_-reh) (to have) with pronouns as subjects. Listing the forms of a verb in order like this is called _conjugating_.

Table 2-1	Conjugating the Verb _Avere_	
Italian	_Pronunciation_	_Translation_
io ho	_ee_-oh oh	I have
tu hai	too _ah_-ee	you (informal, singular) have
Lei ha	lay ah	you (formal, singular) have
lui/lei ha	_loo_-ee/lay ah	he/she/it has
noi abbiamo	_noh_-ee ahb-bee-_ah_-moh	we have
Voi/voi avete	_voh_-ee ah-_veh_-teh	you (formal/informal, plural) have
loro hanno	_loh_-roh _ahn_-noh	they have

See the section "Saying 'you': Formal and informal," later in this chapter, for an explanation of the formal and informal forms in Italian.

We included the subject in this table simply to enable you to see which verb form corresponds to which personal pronoun. Using the verb in a sentence, however, a native Italian speaker would say

> ✔ **Ho un cane.** *(oh oon kah-neh)* (I have a dog.)
>
> ✔ **Hai un cane.** *(ah-ee oon kah-neh)* (You have a dog.)

The rest of the pronouns — he/she/it, we, you (plural), and they — continue in the same manner.

When the subject of a sentence is unclear — for example, when you're speaking about a third person or the sentence is confusing — say the subject. After you name it, however, you then drop the noun or pronoun, as in this example:

> **Luca ha fame. Mangia una mela.** *(loo-kah ah fah-meh mahn-jah oo-nah meh-lah)* (Luca is hungry. [He] eats an apple.)

Coping with Gendered Words (Articles and Adjectives)

The main grammatical difference between English and Italian is that English has only one set of articles for all kinds of words — **a, an,** and **the** — and no gender differences in nouns. Italian differentiates both gender and number. The result is that Italian uses a couple of articles to distinguish between masculine/feminine and singular/plural.

Definite feminine articles

The singular feminine article is **la** *(lah)* (the) — for example, **la casa** *(lah kah-zah)* (the house). If a feminine noun begins with a vowel, you replace the *a* in **la** and the space between the article and noun with an apostrophe, as in **l'amica** *(lah-mee-kah)* (the friend [f]). Most feminine nouns end in *-a.*

The plural feminine article is **le** *(leh)* (the) — for example, **le case** *(leh kah-zeh)* (the houses). You never apostrophize the plural article, though; therefore, it is **le amiche** *(leh ah-mee-keh)* (the friends [f]).

Definite masculine articles

Italian contains more than one masculine article. The most common one is **il** *(eel)* (the), as in **il gatto** *(eel gaht-toh)* (the cat). Its plural form is **i** *(ee)*, as in **i gatti** *(ee gaht-tee)* (the cats).

Italian contains another masculine article: **lo** *(loh).* You use **lo** in the following situations:

✔ With nouns that begin with *z,* as in **lo zio** *(loh dzee-oh)* (the uncle).

✔ With nouns that begin with *y,* as in **lo yogurt** *(loh yoh-joort)* (the yogurt).

✔ With nouns that begin with *gn,* as in **lo gnomo** *(loh nyoh-moh)* (the gnome).

✔ With nouns that begin with *s* followed by a consonant, such as *st, sb, sc,* and *sd* — for example, **lo studente** *(loh stoo-dehn-teh)* (the student).

✔ For nouns that begin with a vowel, such as **l'amico** *(lah-mee-koh)* (the friend [m]). As you can see, you contract the **lo** to **l'** in such a case.

The good news is that the plural article in all these cases is **gli** *(lyee)* (the), as in **gli studenti** *(lyee stoo-dehn-tee)* (the students) and **gli amici** *(lyee ah-mee-chee)* (the friends [m]).

Many masculine nouns end in *-o.* However, many Italian words end in *-e* and can be either feminine or masculine.

The indefinite feminine article

Indefinite articles also play an important role in Italian. The indefinite feminine article is **una** *(oo-nah)* (a) — for example, **una casa** *(oo-nah kah-zah)* (a house). If a feminine noun begins with a vowel, contract the article, as in **un'amica** *(oo-nah-mee-kah)* (a friend [f]).

Indefinite masculine articles

Just as Italian contains more than one definite masculine article, it contains more than one indefinite masculine article. The first is **un** *(oon)* (a), as in **un gatto** *(oon gaht-toh)* (a cat). Its plural form is **dei** *(deh-ee)*.

In contrast to the definite article, you don't contract the indefinite article when the noun that follows begins with a vowel. Therefore, if a masculine noun begins with a vowel, it's **un amico** *(oon ah-mee-koh)* (a friend [m]). In this case, the plural form is **degli** *(deh-lyee)*, as in **degli amici** *(deh-lyee ah-mee-chee)* (some friends).

When you need the definite masculine article **lo** *(loh)* (the), the indefinite counterpart is **uno** *(oo-noh)* (a) — that is, **uno studente** *(oo-noh stoo-dehn-teh)* (a student). In this case, the plural form is **degli** *(deh-lyee)*, as in **degli studenti** *(deh-lyee stoo-dehn-tee)* (some students).

Adjectives

The gender feature of nouns extends to other grammatical categories, including pronouns and adjectives. First, we take a look at the adjectives.

Because an adjective and the noun it modifies are grammatically connected, they must match in number and gender. The adjective adopts the number and gender of the noun. If, for example, you use the adjective **bello** *(behl-loh)* (beautiful) to refer to a house, which is a feminine noun, the phrase becomes **una bella casa** *(oo-nah behl-lah kah-zah)* (a beautiful house).

Here are some examples of how adjectives change according to the nouns to which they refer:

- **il ragazzo italiano** *(eel rah-gaht-tsoh ee-tah-lee-ah-noh)* (the Italian boy)

  i ragazzi italiani *(ee rah-gaht-tsee ee-tah-lee-ah-nee)* (the Italian boys)

  la ragazza italiana *(lah rah-gaht-tsah ee-tah-lee-ah-nah)* (the Italian girl)

  le ragazze italiane *(leh rah-gaht-tseh ee-tah-lee-ah-neh)* (the Italian girls)

- Several adjectives end in **-e,** including **grande** *(grahn-deh)* (big). These adjectives are valid for both feminine and masculine nouns. In the plural of both genders, change the **-e** to **-i** — for example, **grandi** *(grahn-dee)* (big).

  il negozio grande *(eel neh-goh-tsee-oh grahn-deh)* (the big shop)

  i negozi grandi *(ee neh-goh-tsee grahn-dee)* (the big shops)

  la casa grande *(lah kah-zah grahn-deh)* (the big house)

  le case grandi *(leh kah-zeh grahn-dee)* (the big houses)

In Italian, the position of the adjective isn't as rigid as it is in English. In most cases, the adjective follows the noun, but some adjectives can stand before the noun. The position of the adjective does convey a slight difference in meaning — placing the adjective after the noun gives it a certain emphasis. Both of the following phrases mean "a small house," but the second example emphasizes the small size.

- **una piccola casa** *(oo-nah peek-koh-lah kah-zah)*
- **una casa piccola** *(oo-nah kah-zah peek-koh-lah)*

Other adjectives change in meaning depending on whether they precede or follow the noun. In these cases, their position is fixed to the meaning. Here are some examples:

✔ **una cara amica** (_oo_-nah _kah_-rah ah-_mee_-kah) (a dear friend [f])

 un CD caro (oon _chee_-dee _kah_-roh) (an expensive CD)

✔ **un certo signore** (oon _chehr_-toh see-_nyoh_-reh) (a certain gentleman)

 una cosa certa (_oo_-nah _koh_-sah _chehr_-tah) (a sure thing)

✔ **diverse macchine** (dee-_vehr_-seh _mahk_-kee-neh) (various cars)

 penne diverse (_pehn_-neh dee-_vehr_-seh) (different pencils)

✔ **un grand'uomo** (oon grahn-doo-_oh_-moh) (a great man)

 un uomo grande (oon oo-_oh_-moh _grahn_-deh) (a big or tall man)

✔ **un povero ragazzo** (oon _poh_-veh-roh rah-_gaht_-tsoh) (an unfortunate boy)

 un ragazzo povero (oon rah-_gaht_-tsoh _poh_-veh-roh) (a poor, not well-off boy)

✔ **l'unica occasione** (_loo_-nee-kah ohk-kah-zee-_oh_-neh) (the one-and-only opportunity)

 un'occasione unica (oo-nohk-kah-zee-_oh_-neh _oo_-nee-kah) (a unique opportunity)

Talking about Pronouns

A _pronoun_ replaces a noun. When you talk about Jim, for example, you can replace his name with **he.** You often use pronouns to avoid repetition.

Personal pronouns

Several types of personal pronouns exist. The most important ones are the _subject pronouns,_ which refer either to the speaker(s) **I** or **we;** the person(s) spoken to, **you;** or the person(s) spoken about, **he, she, it,** or **they.** Table 2-2 lists the Italian subject pronouns.

Table 2-2		Subject Pronouns
Italian	*Pronunciation*	*Translation*
io	ee-oh	I
tu	too	you (informal, singular)
Lei	lay	you (formal, singular)
lui	loo-ee	he
lei	lay	she
esso/a	ehs-soh/sah	it [m/f]
noi	noh-ee	we
Voi/voi	voh-ee	you (formal/informal, plural)
loro	loh-roh	they
essi/e	ehs-see/seh	they [m/f]

Italians often drop the subject pronoun because the verb ending shows what the subject is. Use a personal pronoun only for contrast, for emphasis, or when the pronoun stands alone.

- ✔ Contrast: **Tu tifi per il Milan, io per la Juventus.** (*too tee-fee pehr eel mee-lahn ee-oh pehr lah yoo-vehn-toos*) (*You're* a fan of Milan, but *I'm* a fan of Juventus.)

- ✔ Emphasis: **Vieni anche tu alla festa?** (*vee-eh-nee ahn-keh too ahl-lah feh-stah*) (Are *you* coming to the party too?)

- ✔ Isolated position: **Chi è? Sono io.** (*kee eh soh-noh ee-oh*) (Who's there?/Who is it? It's *me.*)

Pronouns are used, however, to replace a person or thing already mentioned to avoid repetition.

Direct object pronouns

As its name explains, the direct object pronoun is directly connected to the verb and has no need for a preposition. Examples of direct object pronouns in English are

- I saw **her.**
- She called **him.**
- Do you like **them?**
- You don't need **me.**

Surely you're curious to know what these pronouns are in Italian. Table 2-3 has the answers.

Table 2-3	Direct Object Pronouns	
Italian	*Pronunciation*	*Translation*
mi	mee	me
ti	tee	you (informal, singular)
La	lah	you (formal, singular)
lo/la	loh/lah	him, it/her
ci	chee	us
Vi/vi	vee	you (formal/informal, plural)
li	lee	them [m]
le	leh	them [f]

Here are some examples of these pronouns in context:

- **Mi hai chiamato?** *(mee <u>ah</u>-ee kee-ah-<u>mah</u>-toh)* (Did you call me?)
- **No, non ti ho chiamato.** *(noh nohn tee oh kee-ah-<u>mah</u>-toh)* (No, I didn't call you.)

- **Vorrei ringraziarLa.** *(vohr-ray reen-grah-tsee-ahr-lah)* (I'd like to thank you [formal, singular].)

- **Lo vedo.** *(loh veh-doh)* (I see him/it.)

- **La vedo.** *(lah veh-doh)* (I see her/it.)

- **Ci hanno invitati.** *(chee ahn-noh een-vee-tah-tee)* (They invited/have invited us.)

- **Vi ringrazio.** *(vee reen-grah-tsee-oh)* (I thank you [formal and informal, plural].)

- **Li ho visti.** *(lee oh vee-stee)* (I saw/have seen them [m].)

- **Le ho viste.** *(leh oh vee-steh)* (I saw/have seen them [f].)

You contract the pronouns **lo** *(loh)* (him) and **la** *(lah)* (her) before a vowel. Occasionally, you contract **mi** *(mee)* (me), **ti** *(tee)* (you), **ci** *(chee)* (us), and **vi** *(vee)* (you) also. But never use an apostrophe to contract the plural forms **li** *(lee)* (they [m]) and **le** *(leh)* (they [f]).

Indirect object pronouns

Indirect object pronouns may cause you a little difficulty because the indirect object means "for" or "to," which isn't always evident in English. In general, certain verbs dictate the use of indirect object pronouns — for example, **dare a** *(dah-reh ah)* (to give to). Check out Table 2-4 for a list of these pronouns.

Table 2-4	Indirect Object Pronouns	
Italian	*Pronunciation*	*Translation*
mi	mee	for/to me
ti	tee	for/to you (informal, singular)
Le	leh	for/to you (formal, singular)
gli	lyee	for/to him

Italian	Pronunciation	Translation
le	leh	for/to her
ci	chee	for/to us
Vi/vi	vee	for/to you (formal/informal, plural)
gli	lyee	for/to them

Here are some examples of these pronouns in context:

- **Mi hai scritto una lettera?** *(mee ah-ee skreet-toh oo-nah leht-teh-rah)* (Did you write a letter to me?)

- **Ti ho portato un regalo.** *(tee oh pohr-tah-toh oon reh-gah-loh)* (I've brought a gift for you.)

- **Le do il mio indirizzo.** *(leh doh eel mee-oh een-dee-reet-tsoh)* (I give you [formal] my address.)

- **Gli ho chiesto un favore.** *(lyee oh kee-eh-stoh oon fah-voh-reh)* (I asked/have asked him/them a favor.)

- **Le ho dato un bacio.** *(leh oh dah-toh oon bah-choh)* (I gave her a kiss.)

- **Ci hanno telefonato.** *(chee ahn-noh teh-leh-foh-nah-toh)* (They phoned/have phoned us.)

- **Vi chiedo scusa.** *(vee kee-eh-doh skoo-zah)* (I beg your [formal and informal, plural] pardon.)

- **Gli ho dato un lavoro.** *(lyee oh dah-toh oon lah-voh-roh)* (I gave him/them a job.)

Note that these indirect object pronouns stand for, respectively:

- **a me** *(ah meh)* (to me)
- **a te** *(ah teh)* (to you [informal, singular])
- **a Lei** *(ah lay)* (to you [formal, singular])
- **a lui** *(ah loo-ee)* (to him)
- **a lei** *(ah lay)* (to her)

- **a noi** *(ah noh-ee)* (to us)

- **a Voi/voi** *(ah voh-ee)* (to you [formal/informal, plural])

- **a loro** *(ah loh-roh)* (to them)

Therefore, you can also write the first couple of sentences as follows:

- **Hai scritto una lettera a me?** *(ah-ee skreet-toh oo-nah leht-teh-rah ah meh)* (Did you write a letter to me?)

- **Ho portato un regalo a te.** *(oh pohr-tah-toh oon reh-gah-loh ah teh)* (I've brought a gift for you.)

Saying "you": Formal and informal

You probably already know that many languages contain both formal and informal ways of addressing people. In Italian, you use the informal pronoun **tu** *(too)* (you) with good friends, young people, children, and your family. When you talk to a person you don't know well or to a person of higher rank (a superior or a teacher, for example), you should address him or her formally, with **Lei** *(lay)* (you). When you become more familiar with someone, you may change from formal to informal. According to custom, the older person initiates the use of **tu.**

Note that formal pronouns are always capitalized, whereas the informal forms are lowercased. Don't think too much about why; just remember the rule if you find yourself reading or writing in Italian.

Tu requires the second person singular verb form—for example, the conjugation for **essere** *(ehs-seh-reh)* (to be) yields **tu sei** *(too say)* (you are). **Lei** calls for the feminine third person form—regardless of the gender of the person you're talking to—for example **Lei è** *(lay eh)* (you are [formal, singular]).

The following examples show the forms of **you,** using conjugations for the verb **stare** *(stah-reh)* (to be, to stay). Remember that, in Italian, you don't name the pronoun before a verb conjugation because conjugating the verb makes doing so unnecessary (see the section "Setting Up Simple Sentences," earlier in this chapter).

- ✔ Informal singular: **Ciao, come stai?** *(chah-oh koh-meh stah-ee)* (Hi, how are you?)

- ✔ Formal singular: **Buongiorno/Buonasera, come sta?** *(boo-ohn-johr-noh/boo-ohn-ah-seh-rah koh-meh stah)* (Hi, how are you?)

- ✔ Informal plural: **Ciao, come state?** *(chah-oh koh-meh stah-teh)* (Hi, how are you?)

- ✔ Formal plural: **Buongiorno/Buonasera, come state?** *(boo-ohn-johr-noh/boo-ohn-ah-seh-rah koh-meh stah-teh)* (Hi, how are you?)

Asking Questions

In Italian, at least one thing is easier than in English: forming questions. In most cases in English, you need the auxiliary verb **do** to form a question. In other cases, you need a form of **to be** or **to have.** You also have to invert the sentence. For example, "He goes to the movies" becomes "Does he go to the movies?"

In Italian, forming questions is easy. A question has the same structure as an affirmative statement; you identify a question only by the intonation in spoken language and by the use of a question mark in writing. For example:

Luca va a scuola.	**Luca va a scuola?**
loo-kah vah ah skoo-oh-lah	*loo-kah vah ah skoo-oh-lah*
Luca goes to school.	Luca goes to school? or
	Does Luca go to school?

Italian also contains interrogative pronouns (when, where, what, and so on) with which you can start questions. Table 2-5 lists these key pronouns.

Table 2-5	Interrogative Pronouns (Question Words)	
Italian	Pronunciation	Translation
Chi?	kee	Who?
Che?	keh	What?
Cosa?	<u>koh</u>-sah	What? (This is the preferred use.)
Quando?	koo-<u>ahn</u>-doh	When?
Dove?	<u>doh</u>-veh	Where?
Perché?	pehr-<u>keh</u>	Why?
Come?	<u>koh</u>-meh	How?
Quanto?	koo-<u>ahn</u>-toh	How much?
Quale?	koo-<u>ah</u>-leh	Which?

Sample questions using these interrogative pronouns include the following:

- ✔ **Chi è?** *(kee eh)* (Who's that?)
- ✔ **Che ore sono?** *(kee <u>oh</u>-reh <u>soh</u>-noh)* (What time is it?)
- ✔ **Cosa stai facendo?** *(<u>koh</u>-sah <u>stah</u>-ee fah-<u>chehn</u>-doh)* (What are you doing?)
- ✔ **Quando arrivi?** *(koo-<u>ahn</u>-doh ahr-<u>ree</u>-vee)* (When do you arrive?)
- ✔ **Dov'è la stazione?** *(doh-<u>veh</u> lah stah-tsee-<u>oh</u>-neh)* (Where is the station?)
- ✔ **Perché va a Milano?** *(pehr-<u>keh</u> vah ah mee-<u>lah</u>-noh)* (Why are you going to Milan?)
- ✔ **Come stai?** *(<u>koh</u>-meh <u>stah</u>-ee)* (How are you?)
- ✔ **Quanto dura il volo?** *(koo-<u>ahn</u>-toh <u>doo</u>-rah eel <u>voh</u>-loh)* (How long is the flight?)

> ✔ **Quale è l'autobus per il centro?** *(koo-ah-leh eh lah-oo-toh-boos pehr eel chehn-troh)* (Which is the bus to downtown?)

Introducing Regular and Irregular Verbs

What's the difference between regular and irregular verbs? Regular verbs follow a certain pattern: They behave the same way as other verbs in the same category. Therefore, you can predict a regular verb's form in any tense. You can't predict irregular verbs in this way — they behave a bit like individualists.

Regular verbs

You can divide Italian verbs into three categories, according to their ending in the infinitive form. They are

> ✔ **-are,** as in **parlare** *(pahr-lah-reh)* (to speak)
>
> ✔ **-ere,** as in **vivere** *(vee-veh-reh)* (to live)
>
> ✔ **-ire,** as in **partire** *(pahr-tee-reh)* (to leave)

Verbs in these categories can be regular as well as irregular. Table 2-6 shows you the *conjugation* (the different forms) of three regular verbs.

Table 2-6	Conjugating the Regular Verbs *Parlare, Vivere,* and *Partire*	
Italian	**Pronunciation**	**Translation**
parlare	**pahr-lah-reh**	**to speak**
io parlo	ee-oh pahr-loh	I speak
tu parli	too pahr-lee	you (informal, singular) speak

(continued)

Table 2-6 *(continued)*

Italian	Pronunciation	Translation
parlare	**pahr-_lah_-reh**	**to speak**
Lei parla	lay _pahr_-lah	you (formal, singular) speak
lui/lei parla	_loo_-ee/lay _pahr_-lah	he/she speaks
noi parliamo	_noh_-ee pahr-lee-_ah_-moh	we speak
Voi/voi parlate	_voh_-ee pahr-_lah_-teh	you (formal/ informal, plural) speak
loro parlano	_loh_-roh _pahr_-lah-noh	they speak
vivere	**_vee_-veh-reh**	**to live**
io vivo	_ee_-oh _vee_-voh	I live
tu vivi	too _vee_-vee	you (informal, singular) live
Lei vive	lay _vee_-veh	you (formal, singular) live
lui/lei vive	_loo_-ee/lay _vee_-veh	he/she lives
noi viviamo	_noh_-ee vee-vee-_ah_-moh	we live
Voi/voi vivete	_voh_-ee vee-_veh_-teh	you (formal/ informal, plural) live
loro vivono	_loh_-roh _vee_-voh-noh	they live
partire	**pahr-_tee_-reh**	**to leave**
io parto	_ee_-oh _pahr_-toh	I leave
tu parti	too _pahr_-tee	you (informal, singular) leave
Lei parte	lay _pahr_-teh	you (formal, singular) leave
lui/lei parte	_loo_-ee/lay _pahr_-teh	he/she leaves

Italian	Pronunciation	Translation
partire	pahr-<u>tee</u>-reh	to leave
noi partiamo	<u>noh</u>-ee pahr-tee-<u>ah</u>-moh	we leave
Voi/voi partite	<u>voh</u>-ee pahr-<u>tee</u>-teh	you (formal/ informal, plural) leave
loro partono	<u>loh</u>-roh <u>pahr</u>-toh-noh	they leave

You can apply these patterns to every regular verb. Some regular verbs behave a bit differently, but this doesn't render them irregular. In some cases, such as *-ire* verbs, you insert the letters *-isc-* between the root and the ending, as in **capire** *(kah-<u>pee</u>-reh)* (to understand). See Table 2-7 for the conjugation of this verb.

Table 2-7   Conjugating the Regular Verb *Capire*

Italian	Pronunciation	Translation
io capisco	<u>ee</u>-oh kah-<u>pee</u>-skoh	I understand
tu capisci	too kah-<u>pee</u>-shee	you (informal, singular) understand
Lei capisce	lay kah-<u>pee</u>-sheh	you (formal, singular) understand
lui/lei capisce	<u>loo</u>-ee/lay kah-<u>pee</u>-sheh	he/she understands
noi capiamo	<u>noh</u>-ee kah-pee-<u>ah</u>-moh	we understand
Voi/voi capite	<u>voh</u>-ee kah-<u>pee</u>-teh	you (formal/ informal, plural) understand
loro capiscono	<u>loh</u>-roh kah-<u>pee</u>-skoh-noh	they understand

Irregular verbs

Two important verbs that you often use as auxiliary or "helping" verbs are irregular — **avere** *(ah-veh-reh)* (to have) and **essere** *(ehs-seh-reh)* (to be). See Table 2-8 for the conjugations of these verbs.

Table 2-8	Conjugating the Irregular Verbs *Avere* and *Essere*	
Italian	*Pronunciation*	*Translation*
avere	**ah-veh-reh**	**to have**
io ho	ee-oh oh	I have
tu hai	too ah-ee	you (informal, singular) have
Lei ha	lay ah	you (formal, singular) have
lui/lei ha	loo-ee/lay ah	he/she has
noi abbiamo	noh-ee ahb-bee-ah-moh	we have
Voi/voi avete	voh-ee ah-veh-teh	you (formal/informal, plural) have
loro hanno	loh-roh ahn-noh	they have
essere	**ehs-seh-reh**	**to be**
io sono	ee-oh soh-noh	I am
tu sei	too say	you (informal, singular) are
Lei è	lay eh	you (formal, singular) are
lui/lei è	loo-ee/lay eh	he/she is
noi siamo	noh-ee see-ah-moh	we are
Voi/voi siete	voh-ee see-eh-teh	you (formal/informal, plural) are
loro sono	loh-roh soh-noh	they are

Two other common irregular verbs are **andare** *(ahn-dah-reh)* (to go) and **venire** *(veh-nee-reh)* (to come). See Table 2-9 for the conjugations.

Table 2-9	Conjugating the Irregular Verbs *Andare* and *Venire*	
Italian	*Pronunciation*	*Translation*
andare	**ahn-dah-reh**	**to go**
io vado	ee-oh vah-doh	I go
tu vai	too vah-ee	you (informal, singular) go
Lei va	lay vah	you (formal, singular) go
lui/lei va	loo-ee/lay vah	he/she goes
noi andiamo	noh-ee ahn-dee-ah-moh	we go
Voi/voi andate	voh-ee ahn-dah-teh	you (formal/informal, plural) go
loro vanno	loh-roh vahn-noh	they go
venire	**veh-nee-reh**	**to come**
io vengo	ee-oh vehn-goh	I come
tu vieni	too vee-eh-nee	you (informal, singular) come
Lei viene	lay vee-eh-neh	you (formal, singular) come
lui/lei viene	loo-ee/lay vee-eh-neh	he/she comes
noi veniamo	noh-ee veh-nee-ah-moh	we come
Voi/voi venite	voh-ee veh-nee-teh	you (formal/informal, plural) come
loro vengono	loh-roh vehn-goh-noh	they come

In addition, the verb ending *-rre,* as in **porre** *(pohr-reh)* (to put), is exclusively irregular, as shown in Table 2-10.

Table 2-10	Conjugating the Irregular Verb *Porre*	
Italian	*Pronunciation*	*Translation*
io pongo	<u>ee</u>-oh <u>pohn</u>-goh	I put
tu poni	too <u>poh</u>-nee	you (informal, singular) put
Lei pone	lay <u>poh</u>-neh	you (formal, singular) put
lui/lei pone	<u>loo</u>-ee/lay <u>poh</u>-neh	he/she puts
noi poniamo	<u>noh</u>-ee poh-nee-<u>ah</u>-moh	we put
Voi/voi ponete	<u>voh</u>-ee poh-<u>neh</u>-teh	you (formal/informal, plural) put
loro pongono	<u>loh</u>-roh <u>pohn</u>-goh-noh	they put

Presenting the Simple Tenses: Past, Present, and Future

Clearly, people use more than one verb tense. Sometimes you need to report what you did yesterday or outline what you're going to do tomorrow. The past, present, and future tenses aren't high grammar — they're basic stuff.

Past tense

When you speak about something that happened in the past, you usually use the **passato prossimo** *(pahs-sah-toh prohs-see-moh)* in Italian, which corresponds

to the English present perfect tense: I have done.
You also use the passato prossimo in cases where, in
English, you would use the simple past ("I spoke").

The passato prossimo is a compound tense: It consists
of more than one word, as in "I have heard." Here are
some examples in Italian:

> ✔ **Ho ascoltato un CD.** *(oh ah-skohl-tah-toh oon chee-dee)* (I have listened/listened to a CD.)
>
> ✔ **Ho parlato con lui.** *(oh pahr-lah-toh kohn loo-ee)* (I have spoken/spoke to him.)

The structure of the passato prossimo is very similar
to the English present perfect. It's comprised of the
present tense of the verb **avere** *(ah-veh-reh)* (to have)
plus the past participle of the verb that describes
what happened. In the preceding examples, **ascoltato**
(ah-skohl-tah-toh) (listened) is the past participle of
ascoltare *(ah-skohl-tah-reh)* (to listen), and **parlato**
(pahr-lah-toh) (spoken) is the past participle of **parlare** *(pahr-lah-reh)* (to speak).

The past participle is the form of a verb that can also
be an adjective. For example, "spoken" is the past
participle of the verb "to speak." Table 2-11 gives you
the infinitives and past participles of a number of the
verbs that take some form of the verb **avere** *(ah-veh-
reh)* (to have).

Table 2-11	Past Participles Using *Avere*— To Have
Infinitive	**Past Participle**
ascoltare *(ah-skohl-tah-reh)* (to listen)	**ascoltato** *(ah-skohl-tah-toh)* (listened)
ballare *(bahl-lah-reh)* (to dance)	**ballato** *(bahl-lah-toh)* (danced)
comprare *(kohm-prah-reh)* (to buy)	**comprato** *(kohm-prah-toh)* (bought)

(continued)

Table 2-11 *(continued)*

Infinitive	Past Participle
conoscere *(koh-noh-sheh-reh)* (to meet, the first time)	**conosciuto** *(koh-noh-shoo-toh)* (met)
dire *(dee-reh)* (to say/to tell)	**detto** *(deht-toh)* (said/told)
fare *(fah-reh)* (to do)	**fatto** *(faht-toh)* (done)
incontrare *(een-kohn-trah-reh)* (to meet)	**incontrato** *(een-kohn-trah-toh)* (met)
leggere *(lehj-jeh-reh)* (to read)	**letto** *(leht-toh)* (read)
pensare *(pehn-sah-reh)* (to think)	**pensato** *(pehn-sah-toh)* (thought)
scrivere *(skree-veh-reh)* (to write)	**scritto** *(skreet-toh)* (written)
telefonare *(teh-leh-foh-nah-reh)* (to phone)	**telefonato** *(teh-leh-foh-nah-toh)* (called)
vedere *(veh-deh-reh)* (to see)	**visto** *(vee-stoh)* (seen)

Not all verbs require the helping verb **avere** (to have). Most verbs that indicate movement need the verb **essere** *(ehs-seh-reh)* (to be) to build the passato prossimo:

> ✔ **Anna è andata al mare.** *(ahn-nah eh ahn-dah-tah ahl mah-reh)* (Anna has gone/went to the beach.)
>
> ✔ **Carlo è appena uscito.** *(kahr-loh eh ahp-peh-nah oo-shee-toh)* (Carlo has just gone/went out.)

These examples differ from the preceding ones in two ways: The first verb is a present tense form of **essere** *(ehs-seh-reh)* (to be) instead of **avere** *(ah-veh-reh)* (to have), and one past participle ends with **-a** (**andata**) and one ends in **-o** (**uscito**).

The reason for these differences is that in one case the subject is a woman, Anna, and in the other case the subject is a man, Carlo. When the passato prossimo is compounded with the present tense of **essere** (to be), the past participle ends according to the subject:

- Feminine singular *-a* (**andata**)
- Masculine singular *-o* (**andato**)
- Feminine plural *-e* (**andate**)
- Masculine plural *-i* (**andati**)
- Masculine/feminine together plural *-i* (**andati**)

Table 2-12 lists past participles of verbs that indicate movement and use **essere** to build the passato prossimo.

Table 2-12 Past Participles Using *Essere* — To Be

Infinitive	Past Participle
andare *(ahn-dah-reh)* (to go)	**andata/-o/-e/-i** *(ahn-dah-tah/toh/teh/tee)* (gone)
arrivare *(ahr-ree-vah-reh)* (to arrive)	**arrivata/-o/-e/-i** *(ahr-ree-vah-tah/toh/teh/tee)* (arrived)
entrare *(ehn-trah-reh)* (to enter)	**entrata/-o/-e/-i** *(ehn-trah-tah/toh/teh/tee)* (entered)
partire *(pahr-tee-reh)* (to leave)	**partita/-o/-e/-i** *(pahr-tee-tah/toh/teh/tee)* (left)
tornare *(tohr-nah-reh)* (to return)	**tornata/-o/-e/-i** *(tohr-nah-tah/toh/teh/tee)* (returned)

Here we present an aspect of Italian verb formation that may confuse you. In English, you build the past participle of "to be" by adding the auxiliary "to have" — for example, I have been. In Italian, it's different; you form the past participle of the verb **essere** _(ehs-seh-reh)_ (to be) by using **essere** itself. So you say **Sono stata al cinema** _(soh-noh stah-tah ahl chee-neh-mah)_ (I have been to the movies).

Both the verbs **essere** and **stare** _(stah-reh)_ (to be, to stay), when used alone, take **essere** in the passato prossimo:

Infinitive	*Past Participle*
essere _(ehs-seh-reh)_ (to be)	**stata/-o/-e/-i** _(stah-tah/toh/ teh/tee)_ (been)
stare _(stah-reh)_ (to be; to stay)	**stata/-o/-e/-i** _(stah-tah/toh/ teh/tee)_ (been; stayed)

Present tense

The present tense doesn't require much attention; have a look at the simple sentence construction and the verb forms discussed earlier in this chapter.

Future tense

The Italian future tense isn't a compound form as it is in English (I will/I'm going to). The verb form — or more precisely, the verb ending — includes the time marker (will/going to).

For example, examine the verb **parlare** _(pahr-lah-reh)_ (to speak), which belongs to the family of verbs ending in **-are.** When you cut off the ending, the verb stem **parl-** remains, to which you can add endings that indicate the grammatical person and the tense.

For example, the ending for the first person singular future tense is **-erò/-irò.** Adding it to the stem, you get **parlerò** _(pahr-leh-roh)_ (I will speak). In comparison, the first person singular present tense is **parlo** _(pahr-loh)_ (I speak). Here are some more examples:

✔ **Domani saprò i risultati.** *(doh-mah-nee sah-proh ee ree-zool-tah-tee)* (Tomorrow, I will know the results.)

✔ **Lunedì vedrai Marco.** *(loo-neh-dee veh-drah-ee mahr-koh)* (Monday, you will see Marco.)

✔ **Elena partirà domenica.** *(eh-leh-nah pahr-tee-rah doh-meh-nee-kah)* (Elena is going to leave on Sunday.)

✔ **Finiremo il lavoro fra poco.** *(fee-nee-reh-moh eel lah-voh-roh frah poh-koh)* (We're going to finish this work soon.)

✔ **Quando uscirete dalla chiesa?** *(koo-ahn-doh oo-shee-reh-teh dahl-lah kee-eh-zah)* (When will you come out of the church?)

✔ **Verranno da noi in estate.** *(vehr-rahn-noh dah noh-ee een eh-stah-teh)* (They will come to see/stay with us in the summer.)

Chapter 3

Numerical Gumbo: Counting of All Kinds

In This Chapter

▶ Counting on more than your fingers

▶ Referring to years, months, days, and times

▶ Giving directions

▶ Working with money

*Y*ou can't get away without knowing numbers, even in small talk. Somebody may ask you how old you are or how many days you're visiting. Numbers are used in restaurants, for dealing with money, and for finding addresses. This chapter helps you navigate your way through these situations by giving you counting-related vocabulary to work with.

Counting Cardinals

Cardinal numbers are the most basic forms you use to count: 1, 2, 3, and so on. Table 3-1 gives you the cardinal numbers — you can use these numbers to form the ones that we don't include.

Table 3-1	Cardinal Numbers	
Italian	*Pronunciation*	*Number*
zero	<u>dzeh</u>-roh	0
uno	<u>oo</u>-noh	1
due	<u>doo</u>-eh	2
tre	treh	3
quattro	koo-<u>aht</u>-troh	4
cinque	<u>cheen</u>-koo-eh	5
sei	say	6
sette	<u>seht</u>-teh	7
otto	<u>oht</u>-toh	8
nove	<u>noh</u>-veh	9
dieci	dee-<u>eh</u>-chee	10
undici	<u>oon</u>-dee-chee	11
dodici	<u>doh</u>-dee-chee	12
tredici	<u>treh</u>-dee-chee	13
quattordici	koo-<u>aht</u>-tohr-dee-chee	14
quindici	<u>koo</u>-een-dee-chee	15
sedici	<u>seh</u>-dee-chee	16
diciassette	dee-chahs-<u>seht</u>-teh	17
diciotto	dee-<u>choht</u>-toh	18
diciannove	dee-chahn-<u>noh</u>-veh	19
venti	<u>vehn</u>-tee	20
ventuno	vehn-<u>too</u>-noh	21
ventidue	vehn-tee-<u>doo</u>-eh	22

Italian	Pronunciation	Number
ventitre	vehn-tee-_treh_	23
ventiquattro	vehn-tee-koo-_aht_-troh	24
venticinque	vehn-tee-_cheen_-koo-eh	25
ventisei	vehn-tee-_say_	26
ventisette	vehn-tee-_seht_-teh	27
ventotto	vehnt-_oht_-toh	28
ventinove	vehn-tee-_noh_-veh	29
trenta	_trehn_-tah	30
quaranta	koo-ah-_rahn_-tah	40
cinquanta	cheen-koo-_ahn_-tah	50
sessanta	sehs-_sahn_-tah	60
settanta	seht-_tahn_-tah	70
ottanta	oht-_tahn_-tah	80
novanta	noh-_vahn_-tah	90
cento	_chehn_-toh	100
duecento	doo-eh-_chehn_-toh	200
trecento	treh-_chehn_-toh	300
quattrocento	koo-aht-troh-_chehn_-toh	400
cinquecento	cheen-koo-eh-_chehn_-toh	500
seicento	say-_chehn_-toh	600
settecento	seht-teh-_chehn_-toh	700
ottocento	oht-toh-_chehn_-toh	800
novecento	noh-veh-_chehn_-toh	900
mille	_meel_-leh	1,000

(continued)

Table 3-1 *(continued)*

Italian	Pronunciation	Number
duemila	doo-eh-<u>mee</u>-lah	2,000
un milione	oon mee-lee-<u>oh</u>-neh	1,000,000
due milioni	<u>doo</u>-eh mee-lee-<u>oh</u>-nee	2,000,000
un miliardo	oon mee-lee-<u>ahr</u>-doh	1,000,000,000

Every language follows a certain scheme to formulate higher numbers. In Italian, as in English, the higher value precedes the lower one. To say 22, for example, you say **venti** *(<u>vehn</u>-tee)* (20) and then **due** *(<u>doo</u>-eh)* (2) and simply put them together: **ventidue** *(vehn-tee-<u>doo</u>-eh)*. The same is true for higher numbers, like **trecentoventidue** *(treh-<u>chehn</u>-toh-vehn-tee-<u>doo</u>-eh)* (322) and **duemilatrecentoventidue** *(doo-eh-<u>mee</u>-lah-treh-<u>chehn</u>-toh-vehn-tee-<u>doo</u>-eh)* (2,322).

When two vowels meet — this happens frequently with numbers using either **uno** *(<u>oo</u>-noh)* (1) or **otto** *(<u>oht</u>-toh)* (8) as suffixes — you eliminate the first vowel, as in **ventuno** *(vehn-<u>too</u>-noh)* (21) and **quarantotto** *(koo-ah-rahn-<u>toht</u>-toh)* (48).

Unfortunately, every rule has exceptions, and you simply have to memorize some irregular numbers. The numbers 11 to 19 follow their own rules — refer to Table 3-1 to find out how to pronounce them. You can see that up to the number 16, the rule is reversed — the smaller number precedes the larger one. The numbers 17, 18, and 19 follow the larger-number-first rule but are formed in their own ways.

One other technicality to keep in mind is that the plural of **mille** *(<u>meel</u>-leh)* (1,000) is **mila** *(<u>mee</u>-lah),* as in **duemila** *(doo-eh-<u>mee</u>-lah)* (2,000).

Ordering Ordinals

When giving and receiving directions, you need a command of **numeri ordinali** (_noo-meh-ree ohr-dee-nah-lee_) (ordinal numbers). Because ordinal numbers are adjectives, they change according to the nouns they modify. For example, you use the feminine form when referring to **via** (_vee-ah_) or **strada** (_strah-dah_) (street), which are feminine nouns. Table 3-2 includes the ordinal numbers in the masculine form and then in the feminine form.

Table 3-2	Ordinal Numbers	
Italian	*Pronunciation*	*Translation*
il primo/la prima	eel <u>pree</u>-moh/ lah <u>pree</u>-mah	the first
il secondo/ la seconda	eel seh-<u>kohn</u>-doh/ lah seh-<u>kohn</u>-dah	the second
il terzo/la terza	eel <u>tehr</u>-tsoh/lah <u>tehr</u>-tsah	the third
il quarto/la quarta	eel koo-<u>ahr</u>-toh/ lah koo-<u>ahr</u>-tah	the fourth
il quinto/la quinta	eel koo-<u>een</u>-toh/ lah koo-<u>een</u>-tah	the fifth
il sesto/la sesta	eel <u>sehs</u>-toh/ lah <u>sehs</u>-tah	the sixth
il settimo/ la settima	eel <u>seht</u>-tee-moh/ lah <u>seht</u>-tee-mah	the seventh
l'ottavo/l'ottava	loht-<u>tah</u>-voh/loht-<u>tah</u>-vah	the eighth
il nono/la nona	eel <u>noh</u>-noh/lah <u>noh</u>-nah	the ninth
il decimo/ la decima	eel <u>deh</u>-chee-moh/ lah <u>deh</u>-chee-mah	the tenth

These examples show you how to use ordinal numbers in sentences:

> ✓ **È la terza strada a sinistra.** *(eh lah <u>tehr</u>-tsah <u>strah</u>-dah ah see-<u>nee</u>-strah)* (It's the third street on the left.)
>
> ✓ **È dopo il terzo semaforo a destra.** *(eh <u>doh</u>-poh eel <u>tehr</u>-tsoh seh-<u>mah</u>-foh-roh ah <u>deh</u>-strah)* (It's after the third traffic light on the right.)

Talking about Time

Arranging your schedule requires that you know how to talk about months, days, and times of day, as well as the seasons. Talking about the past or the future may mean that you need to know the words for seasons and decades. This section gives you the vocabulary you need.

The four seasons

The fact that both the famous concertos by Antonio Vivaldi and an oh-so-good pizza are named **quattro stagioni** *(koo-<u>aht</u>-troh stah-<u>joh</u>-nee)* (four seasons) is no accident. Both are subdivided into four parts, and each part refers to one season. Table 3-3 gives the Italian word for each of the four seasons.

Table 3-3	The Four Seasons	
Italian	*Pronunciation*	*Translation*
primavera	pree-mah-<u>veh</u>-rah	spring
estate	eh-<u>stah</u>-teh	summer
autunno	ah-oo-<u>toon</u>-noh	fall
inverno	een-<u>vehr</u>-noh	winter

Decades

In Italian, you can't express a decade in just one word—you use a phrase. When you want to say "in the 60s," for example, you have to say **negli anni sessanta** (_neh-lyee ahn-nee sehs-sahn-tah_), which literally means "in the years 60." You form all the other decades by using this method, like this:

- ✔ **negli anni settanta** (_neh-lyee ahn-nee seht-tahn-tah_) (in the 70s)
- ✔ **negli anni ottanta** (_neh-lyee ahn-nee oht-tahn-tah_) (in the 80s)
- ✔ **negli anni novanta** (_neh-lyee ahn-nee noh-vahn-tah_) (in the 90s)

Months of the year

Whether you're telling someone when your birthday is or planning a vacation, you need to know the words for the months of the year. Note that in Italian, you generally don't capitalize these words, as shown in Table 3-4. When writing dates, especially in official documents, however, capitalizing these words is appropriate.

Table 3-4	Months	
Italian	**Pronunciation**	**Translation**
gennaio	gehn-_nah_-ee-oh	January
febbraio	fehb-_brah_-ee-oh	February
marzo	_mahr_-dzoh	March
aprile	ah-_pree_-leh	April
maggio	_mahj_-joh	May
giugno	_joo_-nyoh	June
luglio	_loo_-lyoh	July

(continued)

Table 3-4 *(continued)*

Italian	Pronunciation	Translation
agosto	ah-<u>goh</u>-stoh	August
settembre	seht-<u>tehm</u>-breh	September
ottobre	oht-<u>toh</u>-breh	October
novembre	noh-<u>vehm</u>-breh	November
dicembre	dee-<u>chehm</u>-breh	December

Days of the week

Making plans with someone is almost impossible without talking about the days of the week. Table 3-5 gives you the days of the week and the abbreviations for them. As with months, you don't capitalize the days of the week in Italian as you do in English.

Table 3-5   Days of the Week

Italian	Abbreviated Form	Pronunciation	Translation
domenica	dom.	doh-<u>meh</u>-nee-kah	Sunday
lunedì	lun.	loo-neh-<u>dee</u>	Monday
martedì	mar.	mahr-teh-<u>dee</u>	Tuesday
mercoledì	mer.	mehr-koh-leh-<u>dee</u>	Wednesday
giovedì	gio.	joh-veh-<u>dee</u>	Thursday
venerdì	ven.	veh-nehr-<u>dee</u>	Friday
sabato	sab.	<u>sah</u>-bah-toh	Saturday

Times of day

You need to know how to communicate about time in order to make an appointment or describe an event. Here are some important time-related words and phrases:

- ✔ **oggi** *(ohj-jee)* (today)
- ✔ **ieri** *(ee-eh-ree)* (yesterday)
- ✔ **l'altro ieri** *(lahl-troh ee-eh-ree)* (the day before yesterday)

  This expression literally means "the other yesterday." The word for "the day after tomorrow" is quite similar.

- ✔ **domani** *(doh-mah-nee)* (tomorrow)
- ✔ **domani sera** *(doh-mah-nee seh-rah)* (tomorrow evening/tomorrow night)
- ✔ **dopodomani** *(doh-poh-doh-mah-nee)* (the day after tomorrow)
- ✔ **alle sette** *(ahl-leh seht-teh)* (at seven)
- ✔ **alle sette e mezza** *(ahl-leh seht-teh eh meht-tsah)* (at seven-thirty; literally, seven and a half)
- ✔ **le otto e un quarto** *(leh oht-toh eh oon koo-ahr-toh)* (a quarter past eight; literally, eight and a quarter)
- ✔ **un quarto alle nove** *(oon koo-ahr-toh ahl-leh noh-veh)* (a quarter to nine)

When you write the time in Italian, you go from 1.00 to 24.00 (or 00.00). But when you speak, you use only 1 to 12. If there's a doubt about a.m. or p.m., you can add one of the following terms:

- ✔ **di mattina** *(dee maht-tee-nah)* (in the morning)
- ✔ **di pomeriggio** *(dee poh-meh-reej-joh)* (in the afternoon)
- ✔ **di sera** *(dee seh-rah)* (in the evening/at night)

Being early or late

Unless you're perfect, you don't always arrive on time, and you may have to communicate that you'll be late or early or apologize to someone for being delayed. The following list contains important verb phrases that you can use:

- ✔ **essere in anticipo** (*ehs-seh-reh een ahn-tee-chee-poh*) (to be early)

- ✔ **essere puntuale** (*ehs-seh-reh poon-too-ah-leh*) (to be on time)

- ✔ **essere in ritardo** (*ehs-seh-reh een ree-tahr-doh*) (to be late)

- ✔ **arrivare/venire troppo presto** (*ahr-ree-vah-reh veh-nee-reh trohp-poh prehs-toh*) (to arrive/to come too early)

The following examples use these phrases in sentences:

- ✔ **Mi scusi, sono arrivata in ritardo.** (*mee skoo-zee soh-noh ahr-ree-vah-tah een ree-tahr-doh*) (I'm sorry, I arrived late.)

- ✔ **Sono venuti troppo presto.** (*soh-noh veh-noo-tee trohp-poh preh-stoh*) (They came too early.)

- ✔ **Meno male che sei puntuale.** (*meh-noh mah-leh keh say poon-too-ah-leh*) (Fortunately you're on time.)

When talking about someone's lateness, you can't avoid the verb **aspettare** (*ah-speht-tah-reh*) (to wait). Following are a few examples using this verb:

- ✔ **Aspetto da un'ora.** (*ah-speht-toh dah oo-noh-rah*) (I've been waiting for an hour.)

- ✔ **Aspetta anche lei il ventitré?** (*ah-speht-tah ahn-keh lay eel vehn-tee-treh*) (Are you also waiting for the number 23 bus?)

- ✔ **Aspettate un momento!** (*ah-speht-tah-teh oon moh-mehn-toh*) (Wait a moment!)

> ✔ **Aspettiamo Anna?** *(ah-speht-tee-ah-moh ahn-nah)* (Should we wait for Anna?)
>
> ✔ **Chi aspetti?** *(kee ah-speht-tee)* (For whom are you waiting?)

Note that the verb **aspettare** takes no preposition, as the English "to wait for" does.

Getting Addresses and Phone Numbers

Knowing your numbers is important when you're giving or asking for contact information, such as a street address or telephone number. Table 3-6 lists some key terms.

Table 3-6	Words Related to Addresses and Phone Numbers	
Italian	*Pronunciation*	*Translation*
indirizzo	een-dee-<u>reet</u>-tsoh	address
codice postale	<u>koh</u>-dee-cheh poh-<u>stah</u>-leh	zip code
numero di telefono	<u>noo</u>-meh-roh dee teh-<u>leh</u>-foh-noh	telephone number
prefisso	preh-<u>fees</u>-soh	area code
fax	fahks	fax
posta elettronica	<u>poh</u>-stah eh-leht-<u>troh</u>-nee-kah	e-mail

Italians have given the @ symbol used in e-mail addresses a fanciful name: **chiocciola** *(kee-<u>ohch</u>-choh-lah)* (snail) or even **chiocciolina** *(kee-ohch-choh-<u>lee</u>-nah)* (little snail) — or you can refer to it in the English way, "at." The Italian for "dot" (as in "dot com") is **punto** *(<u>poon</u>-toh)*.

Talking about streets

As in English, Italian streets are called by different names, and each name incorporates a word meaning "street," "avenue," "boulevard," and so on. You'll find streets named **via, viale, corso,** or **strada.**

What's the difference between **via, viale, corso,** and **strada?** In general, if you want to say "it's a big road," you say **è una strada grande** *(eh oo-nah strah-dah grahn-deh),* although some people use **via** in such a case. A similar concept applies to the words for "avenue": Use **il viale** *(eel vee-ah-leh)* when you mean a wide, tree-lined avenue or boulevard and **il corso** *(eel kohr-soh)* when you include the avenue's name or you mean a street in a shopping district.

Describing your home

People usually refer to their **appartamento** *(ahp-pahr-tah-mehn-toh)* (apartment) as their **casa** *(kah-zah)* (house). For terms relating to flats and houses, read this excerpt from an essay by a little girl from primary school.

Casa mia è la più bella del mondo.
kah-zah mee-ah eh lah pee-oo behl-lah dehl mohn-doh
My home is the most beautiful in the world.

È grande, con tante finestre e due terrazze.
eh grahn-deh kohn tahn-teh fee-neh-streh eh doo-eh tehr-raht-tseh
It's big, with many windows and two terraces.

Il palazzo non è tanto grande, ha quattro piani.
eel pah-laht-tsoh nohn eh tahn-toh grahn-deh ah koo-aht-troh pee-ah-nee
The building is not very big; it has four floors.

Io abito al secondo.
ee-oh ah-bee-toh ahl seh-kohn-doh
I live on the second (floor).

C'è un bel giardino.
cheh oon behl jahr-dee-noh
There is a beautiful garden.

Using the verbs "vivere" and "abitare"

In Italian, two words mean "to live." Although you can use either, you should be aware of a few subtle differences:

- **vivere** (*vee-veh-reh*) (to live) is generally used in the sense of being alive, and to say that you have lived in a place for a long time. You wouldn't use this verb to talk about where you stayed on your vacation, but to tell where your home is.

- **abitare** (*ah-bee-tah-reh*) (to live; to stay) is used to indicate which street you live on.

Table 3-7 shows the conjugations.

Table 3-7	Conjugating the Verbs *Vivere* and *Abitare*	
Italian	*Pronunciation*	*Translation*
vivere	**vee-veh-reh**	**to live**
io vivo	ee-oh vee-voh	I live
tu vivi	too vee-vee	you (informal, singular) live
Lei vive	lay vee-veh	you (formal, singular) live
lui/lei vive	loo-ee/lay vee-veh	he/she lives
noi viviamo	noh-ee vee-vee-ah-moh	we live
Voi/voi vivete	voh-ee vee-veh-teh	you (formal/informal, plural) live
loro vivono	loh-roh vee-voh-noh	they live

(continued)

Table 3-7 *(continued)*

Italian	Pronunciation	Translation
abitare	**ah-bee-<u>tah</u>-reh**	**to live; to stay**
io abito	<u>ee</u>-oh <u>ah</u>-bee-toh	I live
tu abiti	too <u>ah</u>-bee-tee	you (informal, singular) live
Lei abita	lay <u>ah</u>-bee-tah	you (formal, singular) live
lui/lei abita	<u>loo</u>-ee/lay <u>ah</u>-bee-tah	he/she lives
noi abitiamo	<u>noh</u>-ee ah-bee-tee-<u>ah</u>-moh	we live
Voi/voi abitate	<u>voh</u>-ee ah-bee-<u>tah</u>-teh	you (formal/informal, plural) live
loro abitano	<u>loh</u>-roh <u>ah</u>-bee-tah-noh	they live

If you're visiting a city and you want to tell someone where you're staying, use **abitare.** You can also say

- ✔ **Sono all'albergo "Quattro Stagioni"** *(<u>soh</u>-noh <u>ahl</u>-lahl-<u>behr</u>-goh koo-<u>aht</u>-troh stah-<u>joh</u>-nee)* (I am at the hotel Quattro Stagioni.)
- ✔ **Stiamo all'albergo "Il giardino"** *(stee-<u>ah</u>-moh <u>ahl</u>-lahl-<u>behr</u>-goh eel jahr-<u>dee</u>-noh)* (We are staying at the hotel Il Giardino.)

Money, Money, Money

On the one hand, you can never have enough money; on the other hand, money can cause trouble — particularly when you're dealing with foreign currency. This section covers all the words you need to know to deal with basic financial matters.

Going to the bank

You may need to go to the bank for several reasons:

- ✔ **cambiare dollari** *(kahm-bee-ah-reh dohl-lah-ree)* (to change dollars)
- ✔ **aprire un conto** *(ah-pree-reh oon kohn-toh)* (to open an account)
- ✔ **prelevare soldi** *(preh-leh-vah-reh sohl-dee)* (to withdraw money)
- ✔ **versare soldi sul proprio conto** *(vehr-sah-reh sohl-dee sool proh-pree-oh kohn-toh)* (to deposit money into your account)
- ✔ **contrarre un prestito** *(kohn-trahr-reh oon preh-stee-toh)* (to take out a loan)
- ✔ **riscuotere un assegno** *(ree-skoo-oh-teh-reh oon ahs-seh-nyoh)* (to cash a check)

Here are some phrases you may find helpful when you talk with **un impiegato/un'impiegata della banca** *(oon eem-pee-eh-gah-toh/oon-eem-pee-eh-gah-tah dehl-lah bahn-kah)* (a male/female bank employee):

- ✔ **Vorrei aprire un conto corrente.** *(vohr-ray ah-pree-reh oon kohn-toh kohr-rehn-teh)* (I'd like to open an account.)
- ✔ **Vorrei riscuotere un assegno.** *(vohr-ray ree-skoo-oh-teh-reh oon ahs-seh-nyoh)* (I'd like to cash a check.)
- ✔ **Mi dispiace, il Suo conto è scoperto.** *(mee dee-spee-ah-cheh eel soo-oh kohn-toh eh skoh-pehr-toh)* (I'm sorry, your account is overdrawn.)
- ✔ **Può girare l'assegno per favore?** *(poo-oh jee-rah-reh lahs-seh-nyoh pehr fah-voh-reh)* (Could you endorse the check, please?)
- ✔ **Avrei bisogno di un prestito.** *(ah-vray bee-zoh-nyoh dee oon preh-stee-toh)* (I need a loan.)
- ✔ **Com'è il tasso d'interesse?** *(koh-meh eel tahs-soh deen-teh-rehs-seh)* (What is the interest rate?)

When you're in the lucky situation of having money left, you may want to invest it. Table 3-8 gives the conjugation of **investire** (een-veh-*stee*-reh) (to invest).

Table 3-8	Conjugating the Verb *Investire*	
Italian	*Pronunciation*	*Translation*
io investo	*ee*-oh een-*veh*-stoh	I invest
tu investi	too een-*veh*-stee	you (informal, singular) invest
Lei investe	lay een-*veh*-steh	you (formal, singular) invest
lui/lei investe	*loo*-ee/lay een-*veh*-steh	he/she invests
noi investiamo	*noh*-ee een-veh-stee-*ah*-moh	we invest
Voi/voi investite	*voh*-ee een-veh-*stee*-teh	you (formal/informal, plural) invest
loro investono	*loh*-roh een-*veh*-stoh-noh	they invest

Words to Know

conto [m] corrente	*kohn*-toh kohr-*rehn*-teh	checking account
libretto [m] degli assegni	lee-*breht*-toh *deh*-lyee ahs-*seh*-nyee	checkbook
tasso d'interesse [m]	*tahs*-soh deen-teh-*rehs*-seh	interest rate

carta di credito [f]	<u>kahr</u>-tah dee <u>kreh</u>-dee-toh	credit card
ricevuta [f]	ree-cheh-<u>voo</u>-tah	receipt
girare	jee-<u>rah</u>-reh	to endorse
riscuotere	ree-skoo-<u>oh</u>-teh-reh	to cash

Changing money

Whether you're traveling for business or for pleasure, you're likely to need to change money when you travel abroad. If you're in Italy and want to change some dollars into **euro** *(eh-oo-roh)* (euros), you would go either **in banca** *(een bahn-kah)* (to the bank) or to an **ufficio di cambio** *(oof-fee-choh dee kahm-bee-oh)* (exchange office). You usually have to pay **una commissione** *(oo-nah kohm-mees-see-oh-neh)* (a fee).

Nowadays, changing money isn't the most efficient way to get the local currency. In Italy, as in most Western countries, you can find a **bancomat** *(bahn-koh-maht)* (ATM) almost anywhere. Depending on where you shop and eat, you can also pay with a **carta di credito** *(kahr-tah dee kreh-dee-toh)* (credit card) or with **travelers' cheques** *(treh-vehl-lehrs shehks)* (travelers' checks).

You can also use your credit card along with your passport to change money at airports, railway stations, and hotels, but keep in mind that the commission rates in these places are sometimes higher than in banks and exchange offices.

Words to Know

cambiare	kahm-bee-<u>ah</u>-reh	to exchange
il bancomat [m]	eel <u>bahn</u>-koh-maht	the ATM
prelevare	preh-leh-<u>vah</u>-reh	to withdraw
funzionare	foon-tsee-<u>oh</u>-nah-reh	to work; to function
contanti [m]	kohn-<u>tahn</u>-tee	cash
monete [f]	moh-<u>neh</u>-teh	coins
dollari [m]	<u>dohl</u>-lah-ree	dollars

Chapter 4

Making New Friends and Enjoying Small Talk

. . . .

In This Chapter

▶ Meeting and greeting

▶ Describing places

▶ Talking about yourself and your family

▶ Chatting about the weather

. . . .

*W*hen you make contact with people who speak another language, knowing how they say hello and good-bye is especially useful. This chapter explains how to say the very basics in greetings, as well as how to supplement a greeting with a little small talk.

Looking at Common Greetings and Good-byes

To give you a good start in greeting people in Italian, we want to familiarize you with the most common greetings and good-byes, followed by examples:

> ✔ **Ciao!** (*chah-oh*) (Hello and good-bye, informal)
>
> **Ciao, Claudio!** (*chah-oh klah-oo-dee-oh*) (Hello, Claudio!)
>
> ✔ **Salve!** (*sahl-veh*) (Hello and good-bye, neutral/ formal)

Salve, ragazzi! *(sahl-veh rah-gaht-tsee)* (Hi, folks!)

Salve is a relic from Latin. In Caesar's time, the Romans used it a lot.

✔ **Buongiorno/Buon giorno** *(boo-ohn-johr-noh)* [Good morning (literally, Good day), formal]

Buongiorno, signora Bruni! *(boo-ohn-johr-noh see-nyoh-rah broo-nee)* (Good morning, Mrs. Bruni!)

Buongiorno is the most formal greeting. Whenever you're in doubt, use this word. It also means "good-bye."

✔ **Buonasera/Buona sera** *(boo-oh-nah-seh-rah)* (Good afternoon, good evening, formal)

Buonasera, signor Rossi! *(boo-oh-nah-seh-rah see-nyohr rohs-see)* (Good afternoon, Mr. Rossi!)

You use **buonasera** to say both hello and good-bye after approximately 5 p.m. in the autumn and winter and after 6 p.m. in the spring and summer. Just mind the time of day! When in doubt, say **buongiorno** if the sun is still out.

✔ **Buonanotte** *(boo-oh-nah-noht-teh)* (Good-night)

Buonanotte, amici! *(boo-oh-nah-noht-teh ah-mee-chee)* (Good-night, friends!)

✔ **Buona giornata!** *(boo-oh-nah johr-nah-tah)* (Have a nice day!)

You often use this phrase when you're leaving somebody or saying good-bye on the phone.

✔ **Buona serata!** *(boo-oh-nah seh-rah-tah)* (Have a nice evening!)

Like **buona giornata,** you use **buona serata** when you're leaving someone or saying good-bye on the phone. The difference is that you use **buona serata** just before or after sunset.

✔ **Addìo** *(ahd-dee-oh)* (Good-bye, farewell)

Addìo, amore mio! *(ahd-dee-oh ah-moh-reh mee-oh)* (Farewell, my love!)

Addìo is more literary; that is, you see it more frequently in writing than in speech.

✔ **Arrivederci** *(ahr-ree-veh-dehr-chee)* (Good-bye)

Arrivederci, signora Eva! *(ahr-ree-veh-dehr-chee see-nyoh-rah eh-vah)* (Good-bye, Mrs. Eva!)

Deciding whether to address someone formally or informally

As Chapter 2 explains, you have two different ways to address people in Italian: formally and informally.

✔ You generally use the formal form — **Lei** *(lay)* (you, formal singular) — with people you don't know: businesspeople, officials, and persons of higher rank, such as supervisors and teachers. The exceptions are with children and among young people; in those cases, you use the informal.

✔ When you get to know someone better, depending on your relationship, you may switch to the informal form of address — **tu** *(too)* (you, informal singular). You also use the informal with members of your family and with children. Young people speak informally among themselves, too.

Responding to a greeting

In English, you often say "How are you?" as a way of saying "Hello" — you don't expect an answer. In Italian, however, this is not the case; you must respond with an answer. The following are common ways to reply to greetings.

Formal greeting and reply:

Buongiorno, signora, come sta?
boo-ohn-johr-noh see-nyoh-rah koh-meh stah
Hello, ma'am, how are you?

Benissimo, grazie, e Lei?
beh-nees-see-moh grah-tsee-eh eh lay
Great, thank you, and you?

Informal greeting and reply:

>**Ciao, Roberto, come stai?**
>_chah_-oh roh-_behr_-toh _koh_-meh _stah_-ee
>Hi, Roberto, how are you?

>**Bene, grazie.**
>_beh_-neh _grah_-tsee-eh
>Fine, thanks.

Another typical, rather informal, greeting and reply:

>**Come va?**
>_koh_-me vah
>How are things?

>**Non c'è male.**
>nohn cheh _mah_-leh
>Not bad.

Specifying your reuniting

You may want to specify your next meeting when you leave someone. The following common expressions can also be used as good-byes on their own:

>✔ **A presto!** _(ah prehs-toh)_ (See you soon!)
>
>✔ **A dopo!** _(ah doh-poh)_ (See you later!)
>
>✔ **A domani!** _(ah doh-mah-nee)_ (See you tomorrow!)
>
>✔ **Ci vediamo!** _(chee veh-dee-ah-moh)_ (See you!)

Although the short form will usually suffice, you can combine **Ci vediamo** with the other phrases. For example:

>✔ **Ci vediamo presto!** _(chee veh-dee-ah-moh prehs-toh)_ (See you soon!)
>
>✔ **Ci vediamo dopo!** _(chee veh-dee-ah-moh doh-poh)_ (See you later!)
>
>✔ **Ci vediamo domani!** _(chee veh-dee-ah-moh doh-mah-nee)_ (See you tomorrow!)

To this basic phrase, you can also add a weekday or a time — for example, **Ci vediamo lunedì alle cinque** *(chee veh-dee-ah-moh loo-neh-dee ahl-leh cheen-koo-eh)* (See you Monday at 5.) See Chapter 3 for the words for times of day and days of the week.

Words to Know

buongiorno	boo-ohn-johr-noh	good morning; good-bye
ciao	chah-oh	hello and good-bye
Come sta?	koh-meh stah	How are you?
bene	beh-neh	fine
arrivederci	ahr-ree-veh-dehr-chee	good-bye
Ci vediamo!	chee veh-dee-ah-moh	See you!
grazie	grah-tsee-eh	thank you

Finding Out Whether Someone Speaks English

When you meet someone from another country, your first question is probably "Do you speak English?" To ask whether someone speaks English, you need to be familiar with the verb **parlare** *(pahr-lah-reh)* (to speak; to talk). Table 4-1 shows the conjugation of this verb.

Table 4-1	Conjugating the Verb *Parlare*	
Italian	*Pronunciation*	*Translation*
io parlo	<u>ee</u>-oh <u>pahr</u>-loh	I speak
tu parli	too <u>pahr</u>-lee	you (informal, singular) speak
Lei parla	lay <u>pahr</u>-lah	you (formal, singular) speak
lui/lei parla	<u>loo</u>-ee/lay <u>pahr</u>-lah	he/she speaks
noi parliamo	<u>noh</u>-ee pahr-lee-<u>ah</u>-moh	we speak
Voi/voi parlate	<u>voh</u>-ee pahr-<u>lah</u>-teh	you (formal/informal, plural) speak
loro parlano	<u>loh</u>-roh <u>pahr</u>-lah-noh	they speak

Following are some examples of **parlare** in action:

- **Parlo molto e volentieri!** *(<u>pahr</u>-loh <u>mohl</u>-toh eh voh-lehn-tee-<u>eh</u>-ree)* (I like to talk!/I am quite talkative!)

- **Parli con me?** *(<u>pahr</u>-lee kohn meh)* (Are you speaking/talking to me?)

- **Parli inglese?** *(<u>pahr</u>-lee een-<u>gleh</u>-zeh)* (Do you speak English?)

- **Oggi parliamo di musica americana.** *(<u>ohj</u>-jee pahr-lee-<u>ah</u>-moh dee <u>moo</u>-zee-kah ah-meh-ree-<u>kah</u>-nah)* (Today we talk about American music.)

- **Parlano sempre di viaggi!** *(<u>pahr</u>-lah-noh <u>sehm</u>-preh dee vee-<u>ahj</u>-jee)* (They always talk about trips!)

Italians have a nice saying: **Parla come mangi!** *(<u>pahr</u>-lah <u>koh</u>-meh <u>mahn</u>-jee)* (Speak the way you eat!) You may want to say this to someone who speaks in a very sophisticated fashion with a touch of arrogance. This phrase reminds people to speak normally — just the way they eat.

Begging Your Pardon?

When you're getting familiar with a new language, you don't always understand everything that fluent speakers say to you, and you often find yourself asking them to repeat themselves. In those instances, the following sentences are helpful:

- ✔ **Non ho capito.** *(nohn oh kah-pee-toh)* (I didn't understand.)
- ✔ **Mi dispiace.** *(mee dee-spee-ah-cheh)* (I'm sorry.)
- ✔ **Che cosa?** (informal) *(keh koh-zah)* (What?)
- ✔ **Come, scusa?** (informal) *(koh-meh skoo-zah)* or **Come, scusi?** (formal) *(koh-meh skoo-zee)* (Pardon?)

If you want to be very polite, you can combine these three expressions: **Scusi! Mi dispiace ma non ho capito.** *(skoo-zee mee dee-spee-ah-cheh mah nohn oh kah-pee-toh)* (Excuse me! I'm sorry, I didn't understand).

Scusa *(skoo-zah)* and **scusi** *(skoo-zee)* also mean "excuse me," and you use them when you need to beg pardon — for example, when you bump into someone.

Making Introductions

Introducing yourself or introducing acquaintances to one another is an important step in making people feel comfortable. In Italian, what you say and how you say it — which form of address you use and whether you use first or last names — depends on how well you know the person(s) you're talking to.

Introducing yourself

Chiamarsi *(kee-ah-mahr-see)* (to be named/to be called) is an important reflexive verb that you use to introduce yourself and to ask others for their names. To get the ring of the verb **chiamarsi**, practice these easy examples:

- ✔ **Ciao, mi chiamo Eva.** *(chah-oh mee kee-ah-moh eh-vah)* (Hello, my name is Eva.)

- ✔ **E tu come ti chiami?** *(eh too koh-meh tee kee-ah-mee)* (And what's your name?)

- ✔ **Lei si chiama?** *(lay see kee-ah-mah)* (What's your/her name?)

    You use the same verb form with **lui** *(loo-ee)* (he) and **lei** *(lay)* (she) — for example, **lui si chiama** *(loo-ee see kee-ah-mah)* (his name is).

As in English, you can also introduce yourself simply by saying your name: **Sono Pietro** *(soh-noh pee-eh-troh)* (I'm Pietro).

Young people forgo ceremony and introduce themselves more casually, though still politely — like this:

Ciao! Sono Giulio.
chah-oh soh-noh joo-lee-oh
Hello! I'm Giulio.

E io sono Giulia, piacere.
eh ee-oh soh-noh joo-lee-ah pee-ah-cheh-reh
And I'm Giulia, nice to meet you.

The following example offers an informal introduction used only in a very casual situation, such as on the beach or at a disco:

Come ti chiami?
koh-meh tee kee-ah-mee
What's your name?

Chiara. E tu?
kee-ah-rah eh too
Chiara, and yours?

Normally, the older person proposes making the switch to the informal form. The older generation tends to be more formal and may not switch to the informal as quickly as younger people do. If you're uncertain, address people formally.

Introducing other people

Sometimes you have to not only introduce yourself, but also introduce someone to other people. The following vocabulary words may be helpful to you in making introductions — check out the section "Talking about yourself and your family," later in this chapter, for more. With these terms, you can indicate the relationship between you and the person you're introducing:

- ✔ **mio marito** (_mee_-oh mah-_ree_-toh) (my husband)

- ✔ **mia moglie** (_mee_-ah _moh_-lyee-eh) (my wife)

- ✔ **il mio amico** (eel _mee_-oh ah-_mee_-koh) (my friend [m])

- ✔ **la mia amica** (lah _mee_-ah ah-_mee_-kah) (my friend [f])

- ✔ **il mio collega** (eel _mee_-oh kohl-_leh_-gah) (my colleague [m])

- ✔ **la mia collega** (lah _mee_-ah kohl-_leh_-gah) (my colleague [f])

To make life easier, Table 4-2 gives the conjugation of the verb **presentare** (preh-zehn-_tah_-reh) (to present/to introduce). Which pronoun you insert in front of the verb depends on the number and relationship of the person to whom you're making the introduction: **ti** (tee) (to you: informal singular), **Le** (leh) (to you, formal singular), **Vi/vi** (vee) (to you, formal/informal, plural).

The pronouns you see before the verbs in Table 4-2 are there only to help you remember the verb forms. You don't actually use these pronouns in conversation.

Table 4-2	Conjugating the Verb *Presentare*	
Italian	*Pronunciation*	*Translation*
io presento	<u>ee</u>-oh preh-<u>zehn</u>-toh	I present
tu presenti	too preh-<u>zehn</u>-tee	you (informal, singular) present
Lei presenta	lay preh-<u>zehn</u>-tah	you (formal, singular) present
lui/lei presenta	<u>loo</u>-ee/lay preh-<u>zehn</u>-tah	he/she presents
noi presentiamo	<u>noh</u>-ee preh-zehn-tee-<u>ah</u>-moh	we present
Voi/voi presentate	<u>voh</u>-ee preh-zehn-<u>tah</u>-teh	you (formal/informal, plural) present
loro presentano	<u>loh</u>-roh preh-<u>zehn</u>-tah-noh	they present

Words to Know

conoscere	koh-<u>noh</u>-sheh-reh	to meet
presentare	preh-zehn-<u>tah</u>-reh	to present/to introduce
mi chiamo	mee kee-<u>ah</u>-moh	my name is
piacere	pee-ah-<u>cheh</u>-reh	nice to meet you

Getting Acquainted

If you get a good feeling about a person you meet and want to get to know that person better, a conversation usually follows the introduction. This section describes some of the subjects you might talk about.

Talking about where you come from

Meeting people from other countries can be educational. Two common questions, phrased here in the formal, are useful to remember:

▶ **Da dove viene?** *(dah doh-veh vee-eh-neh)* (Where do you come from?)

▶ **Di dov'è?** *(dee doh-veh)* (Where are you from?)

The answers are, respectively:

▶ **Vengo da . . .** *(vehn-goh dah)* (I come from . . .)

▶ **Sono di . . .** *(soh-noh dee)* (I'm from . . .)

Into these phrases, you can insert the names of countries, as well as continents or cities. Table 4-3 lists some of the nations of the world.

Table 4-3	Countries	
Country	*Pronunciation*	*Translation*
America	ah-meh-ree-kah	America
Brasile	brah-see-leh	Brazil
Canada	kah-nah-dah	Canada
Cina	chee-nah	China
Francia	frahn-chah	France
Germania	jehr-mah-nee-ah	Germany

(continued)

Table 4-3 *(continued)*

Country	Pronunciation	Translation
Giappone	jahp-<u>poh</u>-neh	Japan
Inghilterra	een-geel-<u>tehr</u>-rah	England
Irlanda	eer-<u>lahn</u>-dah	Ireland
Italia	ee-<u>tah</u>-lee-ah	Italy
Marocco	mah-<u>rohk</u>-koh	Morocco
Portogallo	pohr-toh-<u>gahl</u>-loh	Portugal
Russia	<u>roos</u>-see-ah	Russia
Spagna	<u>spah</u>-nyah	Spain
Svezia	<u>sveh</u>-tsee-ah	Sweden
Svizzera	<u>sveet</u>-tseh-rah	Switzerland

Some countries (those with a final *-a*) are feminine, and others (those with the endings *-e, -o,* and sometimes *-a*) are masculine. Canada is an exception; it's masculine but ends in *-a.* The United States is masculine and uses a plural article because there are many states.

If you want to talk about nationalities, you have to alter the country names a bit. As you say in English, "Are you American?" or "I'm Canadian," you say the same in Italian:

- ✔ **È Americano/a?** *(eh ah-meh-ree-<u>kah</u>-noh/-nah)* (Are you American?)

- ✔ **No, sono Canadese.** *(noh <u>soh</u>-noh kah-nah-<u>deh</u>-zeh)* (No, I'm Canadian.)

Some nationalities are genderless, while others are gender specific. Table 4-4 lists those ending in *-e,* which are both feminine and masculine.

Table 4-4	**Genderless Nationalities**	
Nationality	*Pronunciation*	*Translation*
Canadese	kah-nah-<u>deh</u>-zeh	Canadian
Cinese	chee-<u>neh</u>-zeh	Chinese
Francese	frahn-<u>cheh</u>-zeh	French
Giapponese	jahp-poh-<u>neh</u>-zeh	Japanese
Inglese	een-<u>gleh</u>-zeh	English
Irlandese	eer-lahn-<u>deh</u>-zeh	Irish
Portoghese	pohr-toh-<u>geh</u>-zeh	Portuguese
Svedese	sveh-<u>deh</u>-zeh	Swedish

In other cases, nationalities have feminine, masculine, plural feminine, and plural masculine forms, as shown in Table 4-5.

Table 4-5	**Gender-Specific Nationalities**	
Nationality	*Pronunciation*	*Translation*
Americana/o/e/i	ah-meh-ree-<u>kah</u>-nah/noh/neh/nee	American
Brasiliana/o/e/i	brah-see-lee-ah-<u>ah</u>-nah/noh/neh/nee	Brazilian
Italiana/o/e/i	ee-tah-lee-<u>ah</u>-nah/noh/neh/nee	Italian
Marocchina/o/e/i	mah-rohk-<u>kee</u>-nah/noh/neh/nee	Moroccan
Russa/o/e/i	<u>roos</u>-sah/soh/seh/see	Russian

(continued)

Table 4-5 *(continued)*

Nationality	Pronunciation	Translation
Spagnola/o/e/i	spah-<u>nyoh</u>-lah/loh/leh/lee	Spanish
Svizzera/o/e/i	<u>sveet</u>-tseh-rah/roh/reh/ree	Swiss
Tedesca/o/he/hi	teh-<u>dehs</u>-kah/koh/keh/kee	German

In English, you put the pronoun in front of the verb. Not so in Italian. Because the verb form is different for each pronoun, you can easily leave out the pronoun — you understand who is meant from the verb ending and the context. You use the pronoun only when the subject isn't clear enough or when you want to emphasize a fact — for example, **Loro sono Americani, ma io sono Italiano** (*<u>loh</u>-roh <u>soh</u>-noh ah-meh-ree-<u>kah</u>-nee mah <u>ee</u>-oh <u>soh</u>-noh ee-tah-lee-<u>ah</u>-noh*) (*They* are Americans, but *I* am Italian).

Table 4-6 shows you the conjugation of the verb **venire** (*veh-<u>nee</u>-reh*) (to come), which is helpful to know when you want to tell people where you come from or ask other people where their home is. The right verb/preposition combination in this case is **venire da** (*veh-<u>nee</u>-reh dah*) (to come from), as in **Vengo dalla Francia** (*<u>vehn</u>-goh <u>dahl</u>-lah <u>frahn</u>-chah*) (I come from France).

The preposition **da** (*dah*) takes different forms based on the gender and number of the noun that follows it. You can tell which form of **da** to use from the article (**la, il,** or **gli**) that the noun takes. Here's how it works:

da	+	la	= **dalla**
da	+	il	= **dal**
da	+	gli	= **dagli**

Wondering how you know which article to use? Continue on, dear reader:

- ✔ You use **la** for a feminine, singular noun.
- ✔ Use **il** for a masculine, singular noun.
- ✔ You use **gli** for a masculine, plural noun.

Table 4-6	Conjugating the Verb *Venire*	
Italian	*Pronunciation*	*Translation*
io vengo	<u>ee</u>-oh <u>vehn</u>-goh	I come
tu vieni	too vee-<u>eh</u>-nee	you (informal, singular) come
Lei viene	lay vee-<u>eh</u>-neh	you (formal, singular) come
lui/lei viene	<u>loo</u>-ee/lay vee-<u>eh</u>-neh	he/she comes
noi veniamo	<u>noh</u>-ee veh-nee-<u>ah</u>-moh	we come
Voi/voi venite	<u>voh</u>-ee veh-nee-teh	you (formal/informal, plural) come
loro vengono	<u>loh</u>-roh <u>vehn</u>-goh-noh	they come

The following examples give you some practice with this construction:

- ✔ **Vengo dal Giappone.** (*<u>vehn</u>-goh dahl jahp-<u>poh</u>-neh*) (I come from Japan.)
- ✔ **Vieni dalla Svizzera.** (*vee-<u>eh</u>-nee <u>dahl</u>-lah <u>sveet</u>-tseh-rah*) (You come from Switzerland.)

✔ **Viene dalla Francia.** *(vee-eh-neh dahl-lah frahn-chah)* (He/she comes from France.)

✔ **Veniamo dall'Italia.** *(veh-nee-ah-moh dahl-lee-tah-lee-ah)* (We come from Italy.)

✔ **Veniamo dagli U.S.A.** *(veh-nee-ah-moh dah-lyee oo-zah)* (We come from the U.S.A.)

✔ **Veniamo dal Canada.** *(veh-nee-ah-moh dahl kah-nah-dah)* (We come from Canada.)

✔ **Venite dalla Russia.** *(veh-nee-teh dahl-lah roos-see-ah)* [You (plural) come from Russia.]

✔ **Vengono dalla Spagna.** *(vehn-goh-noh dahl-lah spah-nyah)* (They come from Spain.)

You might ask the following questions to initiate an informal conversation:

✔ **Sei di qui?** *(say dee koo-ee)* (Are you from here?)

✔ **Dove vivi?** *(doh-veh vee-vee)* (Where do you live?)

✔ **Dove sei nato?** *(doh-veh say nah-toh)* (Where were you born?)

✔ **E' la prima volta che vieni qui?** *(eh lah pree-mah vohl-tah keh vee-eh-nee koo-ee)* (Is this your first time here?)

✔ **Sei qui in vacanza?** *(say koo-ee een vah-kahn-dzah)* (Are you on vacation?)

✔ **Quanto rimani?** *(koo-ahn-toh ree-mah-nee)* (How long are you staying?)

Being you, being there: Using the verbs "essere" and "stare"

Essere *(ehs-seh-reh)* (to be) is the most important verb in the Italian language. You use this verb frequently; it's necessary in meeting, greeting, and talking with people. Table 4-7 gives its conjugation.

Table 4-7	Conjugating the Verb *Essere*	
Italian	*Pronunciation*	*Translation*
io sono	<u>ee</u>-oh <u>soh</u>-noh	I am
tu sei	too say	you (informal, singular) are
Lei è	lay eh	you (formal, singular) are
lui/lei è	<u>loo</u>-ee/lay eh	he/she is
noi siamo	<u>noh</u>-ee see-<u>ah</u>-moh	we are
Voi/voi siete	<u>voh</u>-ee see-<u>eh</u>-teh	you (formal/informal, plural) are
loro sono	<u>loh</u>-roh <u>soh</u>-noh	they are

The following examples show you how to use the verb **essere:**

  ✔ **Sei Americana?** *(say ah-meh-ree-<u>kah</u>-nah)* (Are you American?)

  No, sono Australiana. *(noh <u>soh</u>-noh ah-oo-strah-lee-<u>ah</u>-nah)* (No, I'm Australian.)

  ✔ **Com'è Paola?** *(koh-<u>meh</u> <u>pah</u>-oh-lah)* (What is Paola like?)

  È un po' arrogante. *(eh oon poh ahr-roh-<u>gahn</u>-teh)* (She's a little bit arrogant.)

  ✔ **Siete qui in vacanza?** *(see-<u>eh</u>-teh koo-<u>ee</u> een vah-<u>kahn</u>-tsah)* (Are you here on vacation?)

  No, siamo qui per studiare l'italiano. *(noh see-<u>ah</u>-moh koo-<u>ee</u> pehr stoo-dee-<u>ah</u>-reh lee-tah-lee-<u>ah</u>-noh)* (No, we're here to study Italian.)

  ✔ **Dove sono Elena e Sara?** *(<u>doh</u>-veh <u>soh</u>-noh <u>eh</u>-leh-nah eh <u>sah</u>-rah)* (Where are Elena and Sara?)

  Sono in biblioteca. *(<u>soh</u>-noh een bee-blee-oh-<u>teh</u>-kah)* (They are in the library.)

Another verb also means roughly "to be": **stare** (*stah-reh*) (to be there, to stay). **Stare** indicates the current state of affairs rather than an unchanging condition. You also use **stare** to express the way you feel. **Stai bene?** (*stah-ee beh-neh*) means "Are you okay?" and **Maria sta male** (*mah-ree-ah stah mah-leh*) means "Maria doesn't feel well."

Table 4-8 shows you how to conjugate the verb **stare**.

Table 4-8	Conjugating the Verb *Stare*	
Italian	*Pronunciation*	*Translation*
io sto	ee-oh stoh	I stay
tu stai	too stah-ee	you (informal, singular) stay
Lei sta	lay stah	you (formal, singular) stay
lui/lei sta	loo-ee/lay stah	he/she stays
noi stiamo	noh-ee stee-ah-moh	we stay
Voi/voi state	voh-ee stah-teh	you (formal/informal, plural) stay
loro stanno	loh-roh stahn-noh	they stay

The following examples show you how to use the verb **stare**:

- ✔ **In che albergo stai?** (*een keh ahl-behr-goh stah-ee?*) (What hotel are you in?)

- ✔ **State un po' con me?** (*stah-teh oon poh kohn meh*) (Will you stay with me for a while?)

- ✔ **Non sto bene.** (*nohn stoh beh-neh*) (I don't feel well.)

- ✔ **Oggi stiamo a casa!** (*ohj-jee stee-ah-moh ah kah-zah*) (Let's stay home today!)

- ✔ **Daniela sta a dieta.** (*dah-nee-eh-lah stah ah dee-eh-tah*) (Daniela is on a diet.)

Talking about yourself and your family

Small talk often focuses on family: an opportunity to tell a bit about yourself and your home and learn something about the other person's family and home. Table 4-9 gives you the words for family members.

Table 4-9	Family Members	
Italian	*Pronunciation*	*Translation*
madre	<u>mah</u>-dreh	mother
padre	<u>pah</u>-dreh	father
sorella	soh-<u>rehl</u>-lah	sister
fratello	frah-<u>tehl</u>-loh	brother
figlia	<u>fee</u>-lyah	daughter
figlio	<u>fee</u>-lyoh	son
figli	<u>fee</u>-lyee	children
nonna	<u>nohn</u>-nah	grandmother
nonno	<u>nohn</u>-noh	grandfather
nipoti	nee-<u>poh</u>-tee	grandchildren
zia	<u>dzee</u>-ah	aunt
zio	<u>dzee</u>-oh	uncle
cugina	koo-<u>jee</u>-nah	female cousin
cugino	koo-<u>jee</u>-noh	male cousin
cognata	koh-<u>nyah</u>-tah	sister-in-law
cognato	koh-<u>nyah</u>-toh	brother-in-law
nuora	noo-<u>oh</u>-rah	daughter-in-law
genero	<u>jeh</u>-neh-roh	son-in-law

The Italian language doesn't have a neutral term for "brothers and sisters," like the word **siblings** in English. You have to say **sorelle e fratelli** *(soh-rehl-leh eh frah-tehl-lee)* (sisters and brothers). To avoid this long expression, Italians often reduce it to **fratelli.**

In a casual conversation, you're likely to speak about your own family members. For this purpose, you need the adjective **mio/mia** *(mee-oh/mee-ah)* (my), as in the following examples:

✔ **mio fratello** *(mee-oh frah-tehl-loh)* (my brother)

✔ **mia madre** *(mee-ah mah-dreh)* (my mother)

Words to Know

sposata	spoh-zah-tah	married
divorziata	dee-vohr-tsee-ah-tah	divorced
vedova [f]	veh-doh-vah	widow
mio marito [m]	mee-oh mah-ree-toh	my husband
mia moglie [f]	mee-ah moh-lyee-eh	my wife
mio ragazzo [m]	mee-oh rah-gaht-tsoh	my boyfriend
mia ragazza [f]	mee-ah rah-gaht-tsah	my girlfriend

Chatting about the weather

When you're in conversational trouble, you can always talk about **il tempo** *(eel tehm-poh)* (the weather). Because the weather is such a common topic, you must be armed with the necessary vocabulary. Table 4-10 gives some common weather-related terms.

Table 4-10	Weather Words	
Italian	*Pronunciation*	*Translation*
il clima [m]	eel <u>klee</u>-mah	the climate
mite	<u>mee</u>-teh	mild
la temperatura [f]	lah tehm-peh-rah-<u>too</u>-rah	the temperature
freddo	<u>frehd</u>-doh	cold
caldo	<u>kahl</u>-doh	hot
temperato	tehm-peh-<u>rah</u>-toh	temperate
umido	<u>oo</u>-mee-doh	humid
coperto	koh-<u>pehr</u>-toh	overcast
la nebbia [f]	lah <u>nehb</u>-bee-ah	fog
tempo incerto [m]	<u>tehm</u>-poh een-<u>chehr</u>-toh	uncertain weather
piove	pee-<u>oh</u>-veh	it's raining

When you're talking about the weather, the following idiomatic expressions will make you sound like a native speaker:

✔ **Fa un caldo terribile!** *(fah oon <u>kahl</u>-doh tehr-<u>ree</u>-bee-leh)* (It's terribly hot!)

✔ **Oggi il sole spacca le pietre!** *(<u>ohj</u>-jee eel <u>soh</u>-leh <u>spahk</u>-kah leh pee-<u>eh</u>-treh)* (Today the sun is breaking the stones!)

✔ **Fa un freddo cane!** *(fah oon <u>frehd</u>-doh <u>kah</u>-neh)* (It's terribly cold!)

➤ **Fa un freddo/un caldo da morire!** *(fah oon frehd-doh/oon kahl-doh dah moh-ree-reh)* (It's deadly cold/warm!)

Da morire *(dah moh-ree-reh)* (deadly) is a typical expression used for emphasis. You can use it in all kinds of situations: for example, **Sono stanco da morire** *(soh-noh stahn-koh dah moh-ree-reh)* (I'm deadly tired) or **Ho una sete da morire** *(oh oo-nah seh-teh dah moh-ree-reh)* (I'm deadly thirsty).

Piove sul bagnato *(pee-oh-veh sool bah-nyah-toh)* (literally, it rains on the wet) is an idiomatic expression that Italians use when something positive happens to someone who doesn't really need it. For example, if a millionaire wins the lottery, you could say **Piove sul bagnato** to indicate your feeling that you should've won instead.

Bearing gifts

In Italy, it's very common to bring **il dolce** *(eel dohl-cheh)* (sweets) as a small gift when you're invited for dinner. This sweet can be **una torta** *(oo-nah tohr-tah)* (a cake), **gelato** *(jeh-lah-toh)* (ice cream), or something from **una pasticceria** *(oo-nah pah-steech-cheh-ree-ah)* (a bakery). Equally welcome are **fiori** *(fee-oh-ree)* (flowers) or **una bottiglia di vino** *(oo-nah boh-tee-lyah dee vee-noh)* (a bottle of wine).

Chapter 5

Enjoying a Drink and a Snack (Or Meal)

. . . .

In This Chapter
▶ Talking about eating and drinking
▶ Reserving a table and paying for your meal
▶ Getting three meals a day (at least)

. . . .

You're no doubt familiar with a great many Italian foods, like spaghetti, pizza, risotto, and so on. In this chapter, you find lots of vocabulary about eating, and you find out how to say that you're hungry or thirsty (because crying like a baby just isn't cool). We also tell you how to order food in a restaurant, as well as how meals are taken in Italy.

Eating and Drinking, Italian Style

When you're hungry, it's hard to think about anything else. You have a couple of ways to communicate in Italian that demanding feeling in your stomach:

 ✔ **Ho fame.** *(oh fah-meh)* (I'm hungry.)

 ✔ **Andiamo a mangiare qualcosa** *(ahn-dee-ah-moh ah mahn-jah-reh koo-ahl-koh-zah)* (Let's get something to eat.)

Italians enjoy three main meals, as you probably do:

✔ **la colazione/la prima colazione** *(lah koh-lah-dzee-oh-neh/lah pree-mah koh-lah-dzee-oh-neh)* (breakfast)

✔ **il pranzo** *(eel prahn-dzoh)* (lunch)

✔ **la cena** *(lah cheh-nah)* (dinner)

When you're hungry between meals, you have **uno spuntino** *(oo-noh spoon-tee-noh)* (a snack).

You can't talk about meals and dishes without the basic verb **mangiare** *(mahn-jah-reh)* (to eat). Table 5-1 gives the conjugation.

Table 5-1	Conjugating the Verb *Mangiare*	
Italian	*Pronunciation*	*Translation*
io mangio	ee-oh mahn-joh	I eat
tu mangi	too mahn-jee	you (informal, singular) eat
Lei mangia	lay mahn-jah	you (formal, singular) eat
lui/lei mangia	loo-ee/lay mahn-jah	he/she eats
noi mangiamo	noh-ee mahn-jah-moh	we eat
Voi/voi mangiate	voh-ee mahn-jah-teh	you (formal/informal, plural) eat
loro mangiano	loh-roh mahn-jah-noh	they eat

Words to Know

Ho fame.	oh <u>fah</u>-meh	I'm hungry.
la (prima) colazione [f]	lah <u>pree</u>-mah koh-lah-dzee-<u>oh</u>-neh	breakfast
il pranzo [m]	eel <u>prahn</u>-dzoh	lunch
la cena [f]	lah <u>cheh</u>-nah	dinner
uno spuntino [m]	<u>oo</u>-noh spoon-<u>tee</u>-noh	a snack

Thirst is another pressing need, especially on a hot day. To proclaim your need for a drink, say **Ho sete** *(oh <u>seh</u>-teh)* (I'm thirsty). To ask a companion, "Are you thirsty?" say **Hai sete?** *(<u>ah</u>-ee <u>seh</u>-teh)*.

You can't talk about beverages, drinks, and so on without knowing how to say "to drink." Table 5-2 gives the conjugation of the verb **bere** *(<u>beh</u>-reh)*.

Table 5-2	Conjugating the Verb *Bere*	
Italian	*Pronunciation*	*Translation*
io bevo	<u>ee</u>-oh <u>beh</u>-voh	I drink
tu bevi	too <u>beh</u>-vee	you (informal, singular) drink
Lei beve	lay <u>beh</u>-veh	you (formal, singular) drink
lui/lei beve	<u>loo</u>-ee/lay <u>beh</u>-veh	he/she drinks
noi beviamo	<u>noh</u>-ee beh-vee-<u>ah</u>-moh	we drink

(continued)

Table 5-2 *(continued)*

Italian	Pronunciation	Translation
Voi/voi bevete	*voh*-ee beh-*vete*-teh	you (formal/informal, plural) drink
loro bevono	*loh*-roh *beh*-voh-noh	they drink

At home, you may have to order an espresso at your favorite coffee emporium to get the rich, dark brew you crave, but in Italy, you get the same drink by asking for **caffè** *(kahf-feh)*. In Italy, you rarely hear the word **espresso** *(eh-sprehs-soh)* unless **il cameriere** *(eel kah-meh-ree-eh-reh)* (the waiter) says **Un espresso per la signora/il signore** *(oon eh-sprehs-soh pehr lah see-nyoh-rah/eel see-nyoh-reh)* (an espresso for the lady/the gentleman) as an announcement that this espresso is yours.

In summer, you may want your coffee or tea over **ghiaccio** *(gee-ahch-choh)* (ice). Ask for **caffè freddo/shakerato** *(kahf-feh frehd-doh/sheh-keh-rah-toh)* (iced coffee) or **tè freddo** *(teh frehd-doh)* (iced tea).

Of course, people drink more than **caffè.** You can enjoy

- ✔ **cioccolata calda** *(chohk-koh-lah-tah kahl-dah)* (cocoa)
- ✔ **te** *(teh)* (tea)
- ✔ **succhi di frutta** *(sook-kee dee froot-tah)* (fruit juices)
- ✔ **acqua minerale** *(ahk-koo-ah mee-neh-rah-leh)* (mineral water)
- ✔ **aperitivo** *(ah-peh-ree-tee-voh)* (aperitif)
- ✔ **birra** *(beer-rah)* (beer)

  You can have your beer either in a **bottiglia** *(boht-tee-lyah)* (bottle) or **alla spina** *(ahl-lah spee-nah)* (draft).

Italy is famous for its **vini** *(vee-nee)* (wines). Just the sight of a Chianti bottle brings thoughts of candlelight dinners and romance. **Grappa** *(grahp-pah)* (brandy) is a popular Italian liquor.

When you order a drink in Italy, you need to specify how much you want. Use the following words to do so:

- ✔ **Una bottiglia di . . .** *(oo-nah boht-tee-lyah dee)* (a bottle of . . .)
- ✔ **Una caraffa di . . .** *(oo-nah kah-rahf-fah dee)* (a carafe of . . .)
- ✔ **Un bicchiere di . . .** *(oon beek-kee-eh-reh dee)* (a glass of . . .)
- ✔ **Una tazza di . . .** *(oo-nah taht-tsah dee)* (a cup of . . .)
- ✔ **Una tazzina di . . .** *(oo-nah taht-tsee-nah dee)* (a small cup of . . .)

Words to Know

acqua [f]	*ahk-koo-ah*	water
il vino [m]	eel *vee-noh*	the wine
la lista dei vini [f]	lah *lee-stah* day *vee-nee*	the wine list
bianco [m]	bee-*ahn*-koh	white
rosso [m]	*rohs*-soh	red
rosato [m]	roh-*sah*-toh	blush/rose
rosé [m]	roh-*seh*	blush/rose
un bicchiere [f]	oon beek-kee-*eh*-reh	a glass

The Start and Finish of Dining Out

This section discusses the beginning and endings of meals — making reservations and paying the tab. **Buon appetito!** *(boo-ohn ahp-peh-tee-toh)* (Enjoy your meal!)

Making reservations

Unless you're going to a pizzeria or the **trattoria** *(traht-toh-ree-ah)* (little restaurant) down the street, you often need to reserve a table in a nice restaurant. You commonly use these phrases when making a reservation:

- ✔ **Vorrei prenotare un tavolo.** *(vohr-ray preh-noh-tah-reh oon tah-voh-loh)* (I would like to reserve a table.)
- ✔ **Per stasera** *(pehr stah-seh-rah)* (For this evening)
- ✔ **Per domani** *(pehr doh-mah-nee)* (For tomorrow)
- ✔ **Per due** *(pehr doo-eh)* (For two)
- ✔ **Alle nove** *(ahl-leh noh-veh)* (At nine o'clock)

Words to Know

un tavolo [m]	oon tah-voh-loh	a table
prenotazione [f]	preh-noh-tah-dzee-oh-neh	reservation
domani	doh-mah-nee	tomorrow
stasera	stah-seh-rah	this evening

Paying for your meal

When you want **il conto** *(eel kohn-toh)* (the bill), you ask the waiter to bring it to you. Table 5-3 gives the conjugation of the verb **portare** *(pohr-tah-reh)* (to bring).

Table 5-3	Conjugating the Verb *Portare*	
Italian	*Pronunciation*	*Translation*
io porto	ee-oh pohr-toh	I bring
tu porti	too pohr-tee	you (informal, singular) bring
Lei porta	lay pohr-tah	you (formal, singular) bring
lui/lei porta	loo-ee/lay pohr-tah	he/she brings
noi portiamo	noh-ee pohr-tee-ah-moh	we bring
Voi/voi portate	voh-ee pohr-tah-teh	you (formal/informal, plural) bring
loro portano	loh-roh pohr-tah-noh	they bring

The following are some phrases you're likely to use in a restaurant as you're settling up:

- **Ci porta il conto, per favore?** *(chee pohr-tah eel kohn-toh pehr fah-voh-reh)* (Could you bring us the check, please?)

- **Accettate carte di credito?** *(ahch-cheht-tah-teh kahr-teh dee kreh-dee-toh)* (Do you accept credit cards?)

- **Scusi, dov'è il bagno?** *(skoo-zee doh-veh eel bah-nyoh)* (Excuse me, where are the restrooms?)

Having Breakfast

Your first meal of **la giornata** *(lah johr-<u>nah</u>-tah)* (the day) is usually **la (prima) colazione** *(lah <u>pree</u>-mah koh-lah-dzee-<u>oh</u>-neh)* (breakfast).

Many Italians begin with **un caffè** *(oon kahf-<u>feh</u>)* (espresso) at home and stop for another in **un bar** *(oon bahr)* (an espresso bar) on their way to work. They may get **un cornetto** *(oon kohr-<u>neht</u>-toh)* (a croissant) filled with **la marmellata** *(lah mahr-mehl-<u>lah</u>-tah)* (jam), **crema** *(<u>kreh</u>-mah)* (cream), or **cioccolata** *(chohk-koh-<u>lah</u>-tah)* (chocolate) as well.

An Italian bar isn't the same as a bar you go to in the United States or Canada to have a beer or cocktail in the evening. In Italy, you can go **al bar** *(ahl bahr)* (to the bar) anytime during the day. Bars offer espresso, cappuccino, wine, and grappa, as well as light meals. You find these bars on virtually every street corner.

The man behind the counter in a coffee bar in Italy is called **il barista** *(eel bah-<u>ree</u>-stah)* (the barman). He might ask the following questions:

- ✔ **Qualcosa da mangiare?** *(koo-ahl-<u>koh</u>-zah dah mahn-<u>jah</u>-reh)* (Anything to eat?)
- ✔ **Altro?** *(<u>ahl</u>-troh)* (Anything else?)

If you ask for something, the barista may respond with **Certo** *(<u>chehr</u>-toh)* (Certainly).

Words to Know

il barista [m]	eel bah-<u>ree</u>-stah	the barman
certo	<u>chehr</u>-toh	certainly

spremuta d'arancia [f]	spreh-_moo_-tah dah-_rahn_-chah	fresh-squeezed orange juice
caffè [m]	kahf-_feh_	espresso
tazza [f]	_taht_-tsah	cup
tazzina [f]	taht-_tsee_-nah	small cup

Eating Lunch and Dinner

For working folk in most of the English-speaking world, **il pranzo** *(eel _prahn_-dzoh)* (lunch) is an opportunity for a quick break from the job — a chance to get out and pick up **qualcosa di caldo** *(koo-ahl-_koh_-zah dee _kahl_-doh)* (something warm). Italians do it differently. They may eat **un panino** *(oon pah-_nee_-noh)* (a sandwich) from the **alimentari** *(ah-lee-mehn-_tah_-ree)* (food shop) around the corner, but most workers have one to three hours for lunch.

The traditional courses in an Italian lunch are

✔ **Antipasti** *(ahn-tee-_pah_-stee)* (appetizers), usually served cold, range from **verdure miste** *(vehr-_doo_-reh _mee_-steh)* (mixed vegetables) to **frutti di mare** *(_froot_-tee dee _mah_-reh)* (seafood).

✔ **Primo piatto** *(_pree_-moh pee-_aht_-toh)* (first course) is usually the main, filling course of the meal. You may have pasta, **risotto** *(ree-_zoht_-toh),* **riso** *(_ree_-zoh)* (rice) dishes, or **minestra** *(mee-_neh_-strah)* (soup).

A beloved **primo** is **spaghetti con le vongole** *(spah-_geht_-tee kohn leh _vohn_-goh-leh)* (spaghetti with clams), often called **spaghetti alle veraci** *(spah-_geht_-tee _ahl_-leh veh-_rah_-chee).* **Verace** means "genuine, authentic"; in this case, it means "with genuine Neapolitan clams."

✔ **Il secondo** *(eel seh-kohn-doh)* (the second course) generally consists of **carne** *(kahr-neh)* (meat), **pesce** *(peh-sheh)* (fish), or **piatti vegetariani** *(pee-aht-tee veh-jeh-tah-ree-ah-nee)* (vegetarian dishes). **Contorni** *(kohn-tohr-nee)* (side dishes) can be ordered separately.

✔ **La frutta** *(lah froot-tah)* (fruit) is generally the next-to-last course.

✔ **Il dolce** *(eel dohl-cheh)* (the dessert) is something sweet, such as cake, ice cream, pudding, and so on.

Italians often have **la cena** *(lah cheh-nah)* (dinner) at home, but they also eat out. In the evening, you're likely to go to either a pizzeria or a more formal restaurant.

Savoring Italian soups and pasta dishes

When it comes to soups, Italians enjoy several preparations and different tastes. You can have **una minestra** *(oo-nah mee-neh-strah)* (soup) or **una zuppa** *(oo-nah dzoop-pah)* (thick soup). **Il minestrone** *(eel mee-neh-stroh-neh)* (thick vegetable soup) is often made with small pasta as well as vegetables. **Il brodo** *(eel broh-doh)* (stock) can be **vegetale** *(veh-jeh-tah-leh)* (vegetable), **di pollo** *(dee pohl-loh)* (chicken), **di manzo** *(dee mahn-zoh)* (beef), or **di pesce** *(dee peh-sheh)* (fish).

La zuppa *(lah dzoop-pah)* is usually prepared with **legumi** *(leh-goo-mee)* (legumes), **cereali** *(cheh-reh-ah-lee)* (grains), or vegetables. A few of the choices are

✔ **zuppa di piselli** *(dzoop-pah dee pee-sehl-lee)* (pea soup)

✔ **di ceci** *(dee cheh-chee)* (chickpea soup)

✔ **di lenticchie** *(dee lehn-teek-kee-eh)* (lentil soup)

✔ **di patate** *(dee pah-tah-teh)* (potato soup)

✔ **di pomodori** *(dee poh-moh-doh-ree)* (tomato soup)

✔ **di pesce** *(dee peh-sheh)* (fish soup)

Pasta e fagioli *(pah-stah eh fah-joh-lee)* (bean soup), a popular, nourishing specialty from Tuscany, also belongs to this group.

Pasta usually means durum wheat made with flour and water. The different types include

- ✔ **spaghetti** *(spah-geht-tee)* (spaghetti)
- ✔ **bucatini** *(boo-kah-tee-nee)* (thick, tubelike spaghetti)
- ✔ **penne** *(pehn-neh)* (short, cylinder-shaped pasta shaped to a point at each end)
- ✔ **fusilli** *(foo-zeel-lee)* (spiral-shaped pasta)
- ✔ **rigatoni** *(ree-gah-toh-nee)* (short, cylinder-shaped, and grooved pasta)

Pasta fresca *(pah-stah freh-skah)* (fresh pasta) means **pasta all'uovo** *(pah-stah ahl-loo-oh-voh)* (egg noodles), also called **pasta fatta in casa** *(pah-stah faht-tah een kah-zah)* (homemade pasta). To name a few:

- ✔ **tagliatelle** *(tah-lyah-tehl-leh)* (flat noodles)
- ✔ **fettuccine** *(feht-tooch-chee-neh)* (narrow, flat noodles)
- ✔ **tonnarelli** *(tohn-nah-rehl-lee)* (tubular noodles)

When you have a bite of pasta, make sure that it is **al dente** *(ahl dehn-teh)* (literally, to the tooth; it means that the pasta is a little hard, so you really need to use your teeth!).

Using the verbs "prendere" and "volere"

The verb **prendere** *(prehn-deh-reh)* (literally, "to take," but here, to have) is helpful to know when you're talking about food and drinks. See Table 5-4 for the conjugation.

Table 5-4	Conjugating the Verb *Prendere*	
Italian	*Pronunciation*	*Translation*
io prendo	<u>ee</u>-oh <u>prehn</u>-doh	I have
tu prendi	too <u>prehn</u>-dee	you (informal, singular) have
Lei prende	lay <u>prehn</u>-deh	you (formal, singular) have
lui/lei prende	loo-ee/lay <u>prehn</u>-deh	he/she has
noi prendiamo	<u>noh</u>-ee prehn-dee-<u>ah</u>-moh	we have
Voi/voi prendete	<u>voh</u>-ee prehn-<u>deh</u>-teh	you (formal/informal, plural) have
loro prendono	<u>loh</u>-roh <u>prehn</u>-doh-noh	they have

Here are a couple of examples of this verb in action:

✔ **Che cosa prendiamo?** *(keh <u>koh</u>-zah prehn-dee-<u>ah</u>-moh)* (What should we have?)

✔ **Che cosa prendi?** *(keh <u>koh</u>-zah <u>prehn</u>-dee)* (What are you going to have?)

"To want" is another useful verb in a restaurant, café, or bar. The following conjugation shows you the polite form of the verb **volere** *(voh-<u>leh</u>-reh)* (to want). Whereas English has the verb "to like" (as in "I would like a sandwich") that people use when they're being polite, Italian uses a conditional form of the verb "to want" to express politeness. Table 5-5 shows you the conjugation.

Table 5-5	Conjugating the Verb *Volere*	
Italian	*Pronunciation*	*Translation*
io vorrei	<u>ee</u>-oh vohr-<u>ray</u>	I want
tu vorresti	too vohr-<u>reh</u>-stee	you (informal, singular) want
Lei vorrebbe	lay vohr-<u>rehb</u>-beh	you (formal, singular) want
lui/lei vorrebbe	<u>loo</u>-ee/lay vohr-<u>rehb</u>-beh	he/she wants
noi vorremmo	<u>noh</u>-ee vohr-<u>rehm</u>-moh	we want
Voi/voi vorreste	<u>voh</u>-ee vohr-<u>reh</u>-steh	you (formal/informal, plural) want
loro vorrebbero	<u>loh</u>-roh vohr-<u>rehb</u>-beh-roh	they want

Ordering from the menu

With the words **prendo** *(<u>prehn</u>-doh)* (I want) and **vorrei** *(vohr-<u>ray</u>)* (I would like) in your vocabulary, you're well on your way to successfully ordering food or drink. Here are some useful phrases:

> ✔ **Guardiamo il menù.** *(goo-ahr-dee-<u>ah</u>-moh eel meh-<u>noo</u>)* (Let's look at the menu.)
>
> ✔ **Che cosa consiglia la casa?** *(keh <u>koh</u>-zah kohn-<u>see</u>-lyah lah <u>kah</u>-zah)* (What are your specials?)
>
> ✔ **Sono molto piccanti?** *(<u>soh</u>-noh <u>mohl</u>-toh peek-<u>kahn</u>-tee)* (Are they very spicy?)
>
> ✔ **Le prendo.** *(leh <u>prehn</u>-doh)* (I'll have them.)
>
> ✔ **Vorrei qualcosa di leggero.** *(vohr-<u>ray</u> koo-ahl-<u>koh</u>-zah dee lehj-<u>jeh</u>-roh)* (I'd like something light.)

The many meanings of *prego*

Prego *(preh-goh)* has several meanings. When you say it in response to **grazie** *(grah-tsee-eh)* (thank you), it means "you're welcome." But clerks and servers also use it to ask you what you would like or if they can help you. You often hear **prego** when you enter an office or shop. You also use **prego** when you give something to someone. In this case, the word is translated as "here you are." Prego is also a very formal answer when someone asks for permission. Following are a few examples of how **prego** is used:

✔ **Grazie.** *(grah-tsee-eh)* (Thank you.)

   Prego. *(preh-goh)* (You're welcome.)

✔ **Prego?** *(preh-goh)* (Can I help you?)

   Posso entrare? *(pohs-soh ehn-trah-reh)* (May I come in?)

   Prego. *(preh-goh)* (Please.)

✔ **Prego, signore.** *(preh-goh see-nyoh-reh)* (Here you are, sir.)

   Grazie. *(grah-tsee-eh)* (Thank you.)

Words to Know

il menù [m]	eel meh-noo	the menu
consiglia la casa [f]	kohn-see-lyah lah kah-zah	the specials
saporito	sah-poh-ree-toh	tasty
piccante	peek-kahn-teh	spicy
leggero	lehj-jeh-roh	light

Savoring Dessert

After a meal, Italians often have **frutta fresca** *(froot-tah freh-skah)* (fresh fruit), **un dolce** *(oon dohl-cheh)* (a sweet), or even **tutt'e due** *(toot-teh doo-eh)* (both) for dessert. Another favorite is **gelato** *(jeh-lah-toh)* (ice cream) — rich, creamy, and delicious. You can choose between **gelati confezionati** *(jeh-lah-tee kohn-feh-tsee-oh-nah-tee)* (packed ice cream) and **gelati artigianali** *(jeh-lah-tee ahr-tee-jah-nah-lee)* (homemade ice cream). If you choose the latter, you have to decide whether you want it in a **cono** *(koh-noh)* (cone) or a **coppetta** *(kohp-peht-tah)* (cup).

You also have to decide which **gusto** *(goo-stoh)* (flavor) you want, how many **palline** *(pahl-lee-neh)* (scoops), and whether you want it **con panna montata** *(kohn pahn-nah mohn-tah-tah)* (with whipped cream) or **senza panna montata** *(sehn-tsah pahn-nah mohn-tah-tah)* (without whipped cream).

Words to Know

gelato [m]	jeh-lah-toh	ice cream
cioccolato [m]	chok-koh-lah-toh	chocolate
fragola [f]	frah-goh-lah	strawberry
limone [m]	lee-moh-neh	lemon
cono [m]	koh-noh	cone
dieta [f]	dee-eh-tah	diet
soltanto	sohl-tahn-toh	only, just
tutt'e due	toot-teh doo-eh	both

Chapter 6

Shop 'til You Drop!

. . . .

In This Chapter

▶ Finding your way around a store

▶ Getting the right size and color

▶ Shopping for food

▶ Charging it or paying cash

. . . .

*I*taly is famous for its taste and fashion sense, as well as for the **stilisti** *(stee-lee-stee)* (designers) who build on that reputation. Looking at all the well-dressed Italians, you may feel like going shopping so that you can look as good. What better place to shop for gorgeous apparel than in Italy, which leads Europe in fashion and shoe production?

This chapter also covers another Italian favorite: food. From fresh-caught fish to crusty loaves of bread, you can find everything you need at an Italian **mercato** *(mehr-kah-toh)* (market).

So how do you say "shopping" in Italian? You say **fare la spesa** *(fah-reh la speh-zah)* (literally, making the shopping) when you buy food and **fare spese** *(fah-reh speh-zeh)* for everything else. The good news is that you only have to conjugate the verb **fare,** as shown in Table 6-1.

Table 6-1	Conjugating the Verb *Fare*	
Italian	*Pronunciation*	*Translation*
io faccio spese	ee-oh <u>fahch</u>-choh <u>speh</u>-zeh	I shop
tu fai spese	too <u>fah</u>-ee <u>speh</u>-zeh	you (informal, singular) shop
Lei fa spese	lay fah <u>speh</u>-zeh	you (formal, singular) shop
lui/lei fa spese	<u>loo</u>-ee/lay fah <u>speh</u>-zeh	he/she shops
noi facciamo spese	<u>noh</u>-ee fahch-<u>chah</u>-moh <u>speh</u>-zeh	we shop
Voi/voi fate spese	<u>voh</u>-ee <u>fah</u>-teh <u>speh</u>-zeh	you (formal/informal, plural) shop
loro fanno spese	<u>loh</u>-roh <u>fahn</u>-noh <u>speh</u>-zeh	they shop

Departmentalizing Your Shopping

North Americans have access to huge **centri commerciali** (<u>chehn</u>-tree kohm-mehr-chee-<u>ah</u>-lee) (shopping malls), where you can find everything. In Italy, people shop in **grandi magazzini** (<u>grahn</u>-dee mah-gaht-<u>tsee</u>-nee) (department stores), which are tiny compared to American ones.

In any size of department store, signs help you find your way around:

- **entrata** (ehn-<u>trah</u>-tah) (entrance)
- **uscita** (oo-<u>shee</u>-tah) (exit)

- ✔ **uscita di sicurezza** *(oo-shee-tah dee see-koo-reht-tsah)* (emergency exit)

- ✔ **spingere** *(speen-jeh-reh)* (to push)

- ✔ **tirare** *(tee-rah-reh)* (to pull)

- ✔ **orario di apertura** *(oh-rah-ree-oh dee ah-pehr-too-rah)* (business hours)

- ✔ **aperto** *(ah-pehr-toh)* (open)

- ✔ **chiuso** *(kee-oo-zoh)* (closed)

- ✔ **scala mobile** *(skah-lah moh-bee-leh)* (escalator)

- ✔ **ascensore** *(ah-shehn-soh-reh)* (elevator)

- ✔ **cassa** *(kahs-sah)* (cash register)

- ✔ **camerini** *(kah-meh-ree-nee)* (fitting rooms)

Signs pointing to the various **reparti** *(reh-pahr-tee)* (departments) may or may not include the word **da** *(dah)* (for), as in **abbigliamento da donna** *(ahb-bee-lyah-mehn-toh dah dohn-nah)* (women's wear). Other departments you may be interested in include

- ✔ **abbigliamento da uomo** *(ahb-bee-lyah-mehn-toh dah oo-oh-moh)* (menswear)

- ✔ **abbigliamento da bambino** *(ahb-bee-lyah-mehn-toh dah bahm-bee-noh)* (children's wear)

- ✔ **intimo donna** *(een-tee-moh dohn-nah)* (ladies' intimate apparel)

- ✔ **intimo uomo** *(een-tee-moh oo-oh-moh)* (men's intimate apparel)

- ✔ **accessori** *(ahch-chehs-soh-ree)* (accessories)

- ✔ **profumeria** *(proh-foo-meh-ree-ah)* (perfumery)

- ✔ **articoli da toletta** *(ahr-tee-koh-lee dah toh-leht-tah)* (toiletries)

- ✔ **casalinghi** *(kah-zah-leen-gee)* (housewares)

- ✔ **biancheria per la casa** *(bee-ahn-keh-ree-ah pehr lah kah-zah)* (linens and towels)

✔ **articoli sportivi** (ahr-_tee_-koh-lee spohr-_tee_-vee) (sports equipment)

✔ **articoli da regalo** (ahr-_tee_-koh-lee dah reh-_gah_-loh) (gifts)

Talking with a Sales Clerk

When you have a question or need some advice in a store, you turn to **la commessa** [f] (lah kohm-_mehs_-sah) or **il commesso** [m] (eel kohm-_mehs_-soh) (the sales clerk) and say **Mi può aiutare, per favore** (mee poo-_oh_ ah-yoo-_tah_-reh pehr fah-_voh_-reh) (Can you help me, please?).

Avere bisogno di (ah-_veh_-reh bee-_zoh_-nyoh dee) (to need) is a frequent expression in Italian. You use it in any kind of store. The form that you use goes like this:

Ho bisogno di (oh bee-_zoh_-nyoh dee) (I need)

Simply use the appropriate form of **avere** (see Chapter 2) and then add **bisogno di** to the end to say "you need," "he needs," and so on.

If you're just looking and a salesperson asks **Posso essere d'aiuto?** (_pohs_-soh _ehs_-seh-reh dah-_yoo_-toh) or **Desidera?** (deh-_zee_-deh-rah) (Can I help you?), you answer **Sto solo dando un'occhiata, grazie** (stoh _soh_-loh _dahn_-doh oon-ohk-kee-_ah_-tah _grah_-tsee-eh) (I'm just looking, thank you).

Words to Know

vestiti [m]	vehs-_tee_-tee	clothes
abito [m]	_ah_-bee-toh	suit
camicetta [f]	kah-mee-_cheht_-tah	blouse

camicia [f]	kah-<u>mee</u>-chah	shirt
cappotto [m]	kahp-<u>poht</u>-toh	coat
completo [m]	kohm-<u>pleht</u>-toh	skirt or pants and blouse
giacca [f]	<u>jahk</u>-kah	jacket; sports jacket
gonna [f]	<u>gohn</u>-nah	skirt
impermeabile [m]	eem-pehr-meh-<u>ah</u>-bee-leh	raincoat
maglietta [f]; T-shirt [f]	mahl-<u>yeht</u>-tah; <u>tee</u>-shirt	T-shirt
paio di jeans [m]	<u>pah</u>-yoh dee jeans	pair of jeans
pantaloni [m]	pahn-tah-<u>loh</u>-nee	pants
tailleur [m]	tah-<u>lyehr</u>	skirt or pants and jacket
vestito [m]	veh-<u>stee</u>-toh	dress

Sizing Up Italian Sizes

Whenever you go to another country, particularly in Europe, the sizes — called **taglie** *(<u>tah</u>-lyeh)* or **misure** *(mee-<u>zoo</u>-reh)* in Italian — change, and you never know which one corresponds to yours. Table 6-2 gives you the most common sizes.

Table 6-2	Clothing Sizes	
Italian Size	*American Size*	*Canadian Size*
Women's dress sizes		
40	4	6
42	6	8
44	8	10
46	10	12
48	12	14
50	14	16
Men's suit sizes		
48	38	40
50	40	42
52	42	44
54	44	46
56	46	48
58	48	50

Choosing Colors and Fabrics

Knowing some **colori** *(koh-loh-ree)* (colors) is important. Table 6-3 lists the most common colors.

Table 6-3	Colors	
Italian	*Pronunciation*	*Translation*
arancione	ah-rahn-choh-neh	orange
azzurro	aht-tsoor-roh	sky blue
beige	beh-jeh	beige
bianco	bee-ahn-koh	white

Italian	Pronunciation	Translation
blu	bloo	blue
giallo	<u>jahl</u>-loh	yellow
grigio	<u>gree</u>-joh	gray
marrone	mahr-<u>roh</u>-neh	brown
nero	<u>neh</u>-roh	black
rosa	<u>roh</u>-zah	pink
rosso	<u>rohs</u>-soh	red
verde	<u>vehr</u>-deh	green
viola	vee-<u>oh</u>-lah	purple

Two important words as far as color is concerned
are **scuro/a/i/e** *(<u>skoo</u>-roh/rah/ree/reh)* (dark) and
chiaro/a/i/e *(kee-<u>ah</u>-roh/rah/ree/reh)* (light). Don't
worry over all the vowels at the ends of these words.
You use only one of them at a time according to the
gender and case of the noun it modifies:

- ✔ Use **-o** with male singular nouns.
- ✔ Use **-a** for female singular nouns.
- ✔ Use **-i** for male plural nouns.
- ✔ Use **-e** with female plural nouns.

You may want to specify a particular type of fabric
when shopping for an item. Table 6-4 lists some
common fabrics.

Table 6-4	Fabrics	
Italian	Pronunciation	Translation
camoscio [m]	kah-<u>moh</u>-shoh	suede
cotone [m]	koh-<u>toh</u>-neh	cotton

(continued)

Table 6-4 *(continued)*

Italian	Pronunciation	Translation
flanella [f]	flah-<u>nehl</u>-lah	flannel
lana [f]	<u>lah</u>-nah	wool
lino [m]	<u>lee</u>-noh	linen
pelle [f]	<u>pehl</u>-leh	leather
seta [f]	<u>seh</u>-tah	silk
velluto [m]	vehl-<u>loo</u>-toh	velvet
viscosa [f]	vee-<u>skoh</u>-zah	rayon

Accessorizing

Of course, you want to give your outfit that final touch with beautiful **accessori** *(ahch-chehs-<u>soh</u>-ree)* (accessories):

- **berretto** *(behr-<u>reht</u>-toh)* (cap)
- **borsa** *(<u>bohr</u>-sah)* (bag)
- **calze** *(<u>kahl</u>-dzeh)* (stockings)
- **calzini** *(kahl-<u>dzee</u>-nee)* (socks)
- **cappello** *(kahp-<u>pehl</u>-loh)* (hat)
- **cintura** *(cheen-<u>too</u>-rah)* (belt)
- **collant** *(kohl-<u>lahn</u>)* (tights)
- **cravatta** *(krah-<u>vaht</u>-tah)* (tie)
- **guanti** *(goo-<u>ahn</u>-tee)* (gloves)
- **ombrello** *(ohm-<u>brehl</u>-loh)* (umbrella)
- **sciarpa** *(<u>shahr</u>-pah)* (scarf)

Stepping Out in Style

Knowing that Italy is the leader in the shoe industry, you won't find it hard to believe what good taste Italians have in **scarpe** *(skahr-peh)* (shoes). If you travel to Italy, have a look into the various shoe shops. You may well find the shoes of your dreams, whether they be a regular **paio di scarpe** *(pah-yoh dee skahr-peh)* (pair of shoes), **pantofole** *(pahn-toh-foh-leh)* (slippers), **sandali** *(sahn-dah-lee)* (sandals), or **stivali** *(stee-vah-lee)* (boots).

When you try on shoes, you may need to use these words:

- ✔ **stretta/e** *(streht-tah/teh)* (tight)

- ✔ **larga/e** *(lahr-gah/geh)* (loose)

- ✔ **corta/e** *(kohr-tah/teh)* (short)

- ✔ **lunga/e** *(loon-gah/geh)* (long)

Because **la scarpa** *(lah skahr-pah)* (the shoe) is female in Italian, we provide you with only the female endings for these adjectives: **-a** for singular and **-e** for plural.

Italian uses **numero** *(noo-meh-roh)* (number) to talk about shoe sizes, but **taglie** *(tah-lyeh)* or **misure** *(mee-zoo-reh)* (size) to talk about clothes.

Shopping for Food

People do the bulk of their food shopping in a **super-mercato** *(soo-pehr-mehr-kah-toh)* (supermarket). But many Italian cities have street markets and little shops, called **alimentari** *(ah-lee-mehn-tah-ree)*, where you can get everything from **latte** *(laht-teh)* (milk) over **biscotti** *(bee-skoht-tee)* (cookies) to all sorts of assorted **salumi** *(sah-loo-mee)* (cold meats) and **formaggi** *(fohr-mahj-jee)* (cheeses).

You may choose to pick out your **carne** (*kahr-neh*)
(meat) at a **macellaio** (*mah-chehl-lah-yoh*) (butcher
shop), your fresh **prodotti** (*proh-doht-tee*) (produce)
at a farmers' market, and your **pane** (*pah-neh*)
(bread) at a **panetteria** (*pah-neht-teh-ree-ah*) (bakery),
but you can find everything in a supermarket.

Meats

From the butcher shop, you might select items like
these:

- ✔ **agnello** (*ah-nyehl-loh*) (lamb)
- ✔ **anatra** (*ah-nah-trah*) (duck)
- ✔ **fegato** (*feh-gah-toh*) (liver — if not specified, calf liver)
- ✔ **maiale** (*mah-yah-leh*) (pork)
- ✔ **manzo** (*mahn-dzoh*) (beef)
- ✔ **pollo** (*pohl-loh*) (chicken)
- ✔ **vitello** (*vee-tehl-loh*) (veal)
- ✔ **bistecca** (*bee-stehk-kah*) (steak)
- ✔ **cotoletta** (*koh-toh-leht-tah*) (cutlet)
- ✔ **filetto** (*fee-leht-toh*) (filet steak)

Seafood

In Italy, you get good fresh **pesce** (*peh-sheh*) (fish)
when you're close to the sea or a lake. If you happen
on a good **pescheria** (*peh-skeh-ree-ah*) (fish market),
you can order what your palate desires:

- ✔ **acciughe fresche** (*ahch-choo-geh freh-skeh*) (fresh anchovies)
- ✔ **aragosta** (*ah-rah-goh-stah*) (lobster)
- ✔ **calamari** (*kah-lah-mah-ree*) (squid)
- ✔ **cozze** (*koht-tseh*) (mussels)
- ✔ **crostacei** (*kroh-stah-cheh-ee*) (shellfish)

✔ **frutti di mare** *(froot-tee dee mah-reh)* (seafood)

✔ **gamberetti** *(gahm-beh-reht-tee)* (shrimp)

✔ **gamberi** *(gahm-beh-ree)* (prawns)

✔ **granchi** *(grahn-kee)* (crab)

✔ **merluzzo** *(mehr-loot-tsoh)* (cod)

✔ **pesce spada** *(peh-sheh spah-dah)* (swordfish)

✔ **polpo/polipo** *(pohl-poh poh-lee-poh)* (octopus)

✔ **sogliola** *(soh-lyoh-lah)* (sole)

✔ **spigola** *(spee-goh-lah)* (bass)

✔ **tonno fresco** *(tohn-noh freh-skoh)* (fresh tuna)

✔ **vongole** *(vohn-goh-leh)* (clams)

Produce

When you go **al mercato** *(ahl mehr-kah-toh)* (to the market) — and here, we're talking about an open-air farmers' market — you primarily find **frutta** *(froot-tah)* (fruits) and **verdura** *(vehr-doo-rah)* (vegetables). Table 6-5 lists fruits that you can get in **estate** *(eh-stah-teh)* (summer) and in **autunno** *(ah-oo-toon-noh)* (fall), **agrumi** *(ah-groo-mee)* (citrus fruits), and fruits you can get **tutto l'anno** *(toot-toh lahn-noh)* (year-round). We give you the forms in singular and plural.

Table 6-5	Fruits and Vegetables	
Italian/Plural	*Pronunciation*	*Translation*
albicocca/ albicocche [f]	ahl-bee-kohk-kah/-keh	apricot
ananas [m]	ah-nah-nahs	pineapple(s)
arancia/arance [f]	ah-rahn-chah/-cheh	orange
asparago/i [m]	ah-spah-rah-goh/-jee	asparagus
banana/e [f]	bah-nah-nah/-neh	banana

(continued)

Table 6-5 *(continued)*

Italian/Plural	Pronunciation	Translation
broccoli [m]	<u>brohk</u>-koh-lee	broccoli
carota/e [f]	kah-<u>roh</u>-tah/-teh	carrot
cavolo/i [m]	<u>kah</u>-voh-loh/-lee	cabbage
ciliegia/e [f]	chee-lee-<u>eh</u>-jah/-jeh	cherry
cocomero/i [m]	koh-<u>koh</u>-meh-roh/-ree	watermelon
fico/fichi [m]	<u>fee</u>-koh/-kee	fig
fragola/e [f]	<u>frah</u>-goh-lah/-leh	strawberry
fungo/funghi [m]	<u>foon</u>-goh/-gee	mushroom
limone/i [m]	lee-<u>moh</u>-neh/-nee	lemon
mela/e [f]	<u>meh</u>-lah/-leh	apple
melanzana/e [f]	meh-lahn-<u>dzah</u>-nah/-neh	eggplant
melone/i [m]	meh-<u>loh</u>-neh/-nee	melon
peperone/i [m]	peh-peh-<u>roh</u>-neh/-nee	pepper
pera/e [f]	<u>peh</u>-rah/-reh	pear
pesca/pesche [f]	<u>pehs</u>-kah/-keh	peach
pomodoro/i [m]	poh-moh-<u>doh</u>-roh/-ree	tomato
pompelmo/i [m]	pohm-<u>pehl</u>-moh/-mee	grapefruit
prugna/e [f]	<u>proo</u>-nyah/-nyeh	plum
spinaci [m]	spee-<u>nah</u>-chee	spinach
uva [f]	<u>oo</u>-vah	grape(s)
zucchine/i [f/m]	dzook-<u>kee</u>-neh/-nee	zucchini

In most cases, you say what you want and the seller picks it out for you. Prices are according to weight, usually by **chilo** *(kee-loh)* (kilo). Occasionally, you find little baskets or paper bags, which indicate that you can choose your own **frutta** *(froot-tah)* (fruit) or **verdura** *(vehr-doo-rah)* (vegetables).

Un etto *(oon eht-toh)* means 100 grams. **Mezz'etto** *(meht-tseht-toh)* is 50 grams, because **mezzo** *(meht-tsoh)* means "half." Likewise, a **mezzo chilo** *(meht-tsoh kee-loh)* is half a kilo.

Baked goods

In a **panetteria** *(pah-neht-teh-ree-ah)* (bakery), you can try all sorts of different kinds of **pane** *(pah-neh)* (bread), ranging from **il pane integrale** *(eel pah-neh een-teh-grah-leh)* (whole wheat bread) to **dolci** *(dohl-chee)* (pastries).

In most Italian bakeries, you also find **pizza al taglio** *(peet-tsah ahl tah-lyoh)* (slices of pizza), which you buy according to weight. You can choose between **pizza bianca** *(peet-tsah bee-ahn-kah)* (white pizza) — that is, pizza topped only with mozzarella and olive oil — and **pizza rossa** *(peet-tsah rohs-sah)* (red pizza), which is topped with mozzarella and tomatoes or tomato sauce. The flavor can vary from bakery to bakery, as it does from region to region.

Words to Know

gli alimentari [m]	lyee ah-lee-mehn-tah-ree	food shop
la drogheria [f]	lah droh-geh-ree-ah	grocery store

continued

Words to Know (continued)

il fruttivendolo [m]	eel froot-tee-_vehn_-doh-loh	produce store, greengrocer
il mercato [m]	eel mehr-_kah_-toh	market
la panetteria [f]	lah pah-neht-teh-_ree_-ah	bakery
la pescheria [f]	lah peh-skeh-_ree_-ah	fish store
la salumeria [f]	lah sah-loo-meh-_ree_-ah	delicatessen

Paying for Your Purchases

When you want to buy something, you have to pay for it. Therefore, we provide the conjugation of the verb **pagare** (pah-_gah_-reh) (to pay) in Table 6-6.

Table 6-6	Conjugating the Verb *Pagare*	
Italian	*Pronunciation*	*Translation*
io pago	_ee_-oh _pah_-goh	I pay
tu paghi	too _pah_-gee	you (informal, singular) pay
Lei paga	lay _pah_-gah	you (formal, singular) pay
lui/lei paga	_loo_-ee/lay _pah_-gah	he/she pays
noi paghiamo	_noh_-ee pah-gee-_ah_-moh	we pay

Italian	Pronunciation	Translation
Voi/voi pagate	<u>voh</u>-ee pah-<u>gah</u>-teh	you (formal/informal, plural) pay
loro pagano	<u>loh</u>-roh <u>pah</u>-gah-noh	they pay

In Italian department stores, prices are clearly labeled
in euros and include sales tax. Often, during **saldi**
(sahl-dee) (sales), **il prezzo** *(eel preht-tsoh)* (the price)
on the tag is already reduced, but you may find tags
reading **saldi alla cassa** *(sahl-dee ahl-lah kahs-sah)*
(reduction at the cash register).

 When you want to know the price of an item,
you ask **Quanto vengono?** *(koo-ahn-toh vehn-goh-noh)* (How much are they?) or **Quanto
costano?** *(koo-ahn-toh koh-stah-noh)* (How
much do they cost?).

 In Italy, you can't pay by credit card or check
everywhere, so ask before you buy something. Shop doors usually indicate which
cards the establishment accepts; some
establishments welcome neither checks nor
credit cards. Italians generally like to be paid
in contanti *(een kohn-tahn-tee)* (in cash).

The following phrases can help you complete your
purchase:

- ✔ **Posso pagare con la carta di credito?** *(pohs-soh
pah-gah-reh kohn lah kahr-tah dee kreh-dee-toh)*
(Can I pay with a credit card?)

- ✔ **Mi dispiace, non accettiamo carte di credito.
Dovrebbe pagare in contanti.** *(mee dee-spee-ah-
cheh nohn ahch-cheht-tee-ah-moh kahr-teh dee
kreh-dee-toh doh-vrehb-beh pah-gah-reh een kohn-
tahn-tee)* (I'm sorry, we don't accept credit
cards. You have to pay cash.)

- ✔ **Dov'è il prossimo bancomat?** *(doh-veh eel
prohs-see-moh bahn-koh-maht)* (Where is the
nearest ATM?)

Words to Know

accettare	ahch-cheht-<u>tah</u>-reh	to accept
la carta di credito [f]	lah <u>kahr</u>-tah dee <u>kreh</u>-dee-toh	the credit card
il bancomat [m]	eel <u>bahn</u>-koh-maht	the ATM
contanti [m]	kohn-<u>tahn</u>-tee	cash
travelers' checks [m]	<u>trah</u>-vehl-lehrs shehks	travelers' checks
spiccioli [m]	<u>speech</u>-choh-lee	small change

Chapter 7

Making Leisure a Top Priority

In This Chapter

▶ Enjoying the fine arts

▶ Extending and receiving invitations

▶ Discovering the great outdoors

▶ Pursuing sports and other hobbies

*H*itting the town is always fun, whether you're visiting someplace new or playing **il turista** *(eel too-ree-stah)* (the tourist) in your own hometown. In this chapter, we give you the information you need to talk about having fun and socializing with others.

In general, Italians are sociable people who enjoy having a good time. You see them having espressos together **al bar** *(ahl bahr)* (in the bar) or drinks at night **in piazza** *(een pee-aht-tsah)* (on the public square). Most Italians love to go out in the evenings, crowding the streets until late at night. On weekends, Italians like to go out in groups: They meet up with their **amici** *(ah-mee-chee)* (friends) for get-togethers.

Acquiring Culture

No matter where you live or travel to, most major cities have a weekly **pubblicazione** *(poob-blee-kah-tsee-oh-neh)* (publication) that lists information about upcoming events. These publications include descriptions and schedules for theaters, exhibitions, festivals, films, and so on. Of course, advertisements also fill the pages, but the difference between an **annuncio** *(ahn-noon-choh)* (announcement) and **pubblicità** *(poob-blee-chee-tah)* (advertising) is usually easy to determine.

Newspapers aren't your only source of information about things to see and do. Asking the following questions can get you the answers you want:

- ✔ **Cosa c'è da fare di sera?** *(koh-zah cheh dah fah-reh dee seh-rah)* (Are there any events in the evenings?)

- ✔ **Può suggerirmi qualcosa?** *(poo-oh sooj-jeh-reer-mee koo-ahl-koh-zah)* (Can you recommend something to me?)

- ✔ **C'è un concerto stasera?** *(cheh oon kohn-chehr-toh stah-seh-rah)* (Is there a concert tonight?)

- ✔ **Dove si comprano i biglietti?** *(doh-veh see kohm-prah-noh ee bee-lyeht-tee)* (Where can we get tickets?)

- ✔ **Ci sono ancora posti?** *(chee soh-noh ahn-koh-rah poh-stee)* (Are there any seats left?)

- ✔ **Quanto vengono i biglietti?** *(koo-ahn-toh vehn-goh-noh ee bee-lyeht-tee)* (How much are the tickets?)

When you're seeing a show, certain verbs are helpful: **cominciare** *(koh-meen-chah-reh)* (to start) and **finire** *(fee-nee-reh)* (to end). Take a few examples:

- ✔ **Il film comincia alle sette.** *(eel feelm koh-meen-chah ahl-leh seht-teh)* (The film starts at 7:00.)

✔ **Lo spettacolo finisce alle nove e trenta.** *(loh speht-tah-koh-loh fee-nee-sheh ahl-leh noh-veh eh trehn-tah)* (The show ends at 9:30.)

Words to Know

a che ora?	ah keh oh-rah	(at) what time?
quando?	koo-ahn-doh	when?
dove?	doh-veh	where?
spettacolo [m]	speht-tah-koh-loh	show, performance
museo [m]	moo-zeh-oh	museum
mostra [f]	moh-strah	exhibit
biglietto [m]	bee-lyeht-toh	ticket
esaurito	eh-zah-oo-ree-toh	sold out
intervallo [m]	een-tehr-vahl-loh	intermission

Going to the movies

Going **al cinema** *(ahl chee-neh-mah)* (to the movies) is a popular activity almost everywhere. You can go

✔ **da solo** *(dah soh-loh)* (alone)

✔ **con un amico** *(kohn oon ah-mee-koh)* (with a friend)

✔ **in gruppo** *(een groop-poh)* (in a group)

Often, **il film** *(eel feelm)* (the film) you want to see is playing at a **multisala** *(mool-tee-sah-lah)* (multiplex).

In Italy, American films normally are **doppiati** *(dohp-pee-ah-tee)* (dubbed) into Italian, but you can sometimes find the original English version with Italian subtitles.

Following are some common questions about the movies:

- ✔ **Andiamo al cinema?** *(ahn-dee-ah-moh ahl chee-neh-mah)* (Shall we go to the movies?)

- ✔ **Cosa danno?** *(koh-zah dahn-noh)* (What's playing?)

- ✔ **Chi sono gli attori?** *(kee soh-noh lyee aht-toh-ree)* (Who's starring?)

- ✔ **Dove lo fanno?** *(doh-veh loh fahn-noh)* (Where is [the movie] being shown?)

- ✔ **E' in lingua (versione) originale?** *(eh een leen-goo-ah [vehr-see-oh-neh] oh-ree-jee-nah-leh)* (Is the film in the original language?)

- ✔ **Dov'è il cinema?** *(doh-veh eel chee-neh-mah)* (Where is the cinema?)

  Note: **Dov'è** is the contracted form of **Dove è.**

Movie theaters are often crowded. Therefore, reserving your **biglietto** *(bee-lyeht-toh)* (ticket) for a movie in advance is always wise.

Words to Know

attore [m]	aht-toh-reh	actor
regista [f/m]	reh-jee-stah	director
trama [f]	trah-mah	plot
scena [f]	sheh-nah	scene

doppiati	dohp-pee-<u>ah</u>-tee	dubbed
multisala [m]	mool-tee-<u>sah</u>-lah	multiplex

Choosing your seat at the theater

The language of the theater and the cinema is very similar. When you attend a play, opera, or symphony, however, where you sit is more of a cause for discussion. In most cases, seats in the **platea** *(plah-<u>teh</u>-ah)* (orchestra) are **poltronissime** *(pohl-troh-<u>nees</u>-see-meh)* (seats in the first and second rows) and **poltrone** *(pohl-<u>troh</u>-neh)* (seats in the following rows). Or you can choose **posti nei palchi** *(<u>poh</u>-stee nay <u>pahl</u>-kee)* (box seats).

Some theaters indicate seats by the number of the row: **i primi posti** *(ee <u>pree</u>-mee <u>poh</u>-stee)* (first seats) are in the first five or six rows, **i secondi posti** *(ee seh-<u>kohn</u>-dee <u>poh</u>-stee)* (second seats) are in the following ones, and so on.

You may want to avoid certain seats. A doctor who may be called away in the middle of a performance probably doesn't want to sit **centrale/i** *(chehn-<u>trah</u>-leh/lee)* (in the middle of the row). Or maybe you don't like feeling hemmed in and want to choose seats **laterale/i** *(lah-teh-<u>rah</u>-leh/lee)* (on the sides).

In large theaters and in opera houses, you can sit in **il loggione** *(eel lohj-<u>joh</u>-neh)* (the gallery), which is also called **la piccionaia** *(lah peech-choh-<u>nah</u>-yah)* (literally, the pigeon house) because it's high up.

Following are a few useful phrases concerning performances:

- ✔ **la replica** *(lah <u>reh</u>-plee-kah)* (repeat performance)
- ✔ **la matinée** *(lah mah-tee-<u>neh</u>)* (matinee)
- ✔ **lo spettacolo pomeridiano** *(loh speht-<u>tah</u>-koh-loh poh-meh-ree-dee-<u>ah</u>-noh)* (afternoon performance)

Going to a concert

Music is the universal language. Some of the most popular forms, such as **l'opera** *(loh-peh-rah)* (opera), have a close association with Italian.

Maybe you know a musician who plays an instrument in his or her spare time. You're probably curious and want to ask questions (and will hear answers) such as

✔ **Che strumento suoni?** *(keh stroo-mehn-toh soo-oh-nee)* (Which instrument do you play?)

 Suono il violino. *(soo-oh-noh eel vee-oh-lee-noh)* (I play the violin.)

✔ **Dove suonate stasera?** *(doh-veh soo-oh-nah-teh stah-seh-rah)* (Where are you playing tonight?)

 Suoniamo al Blu Notte. *(soo-oh-nyah-moh ahl bloo noht-teh)* (We play at the Blu Notte.)

✔ **Chi suona in famiglia?** *(kee soo-oh-nah een fah-mee-lyah)* (Who in the family plays?)

 Suonano tutti. *(soo-oh-nah-noh toot-tee)* (All of them play.)

Words to Know

musica [f]	moo-zee-kah	music
concerto [m]	kohn-chehr-toh	concert
musicisti [m]	moo-zee-chee-stee	musicians
suonare	soo-oh-nah-reh	to play (a musical instrument)
piano (forte) [m]	pee-ah-noh (-fohr-teh)	piano

Inviting Fun

Getting or giving **un invito** *(oon een-vee-toh)* (an invitation) is always a pleasure, whether you invite a friend to a casual dinner or receive an invitation to what promises to be **la festa** *(lah feh-stah)* (the party) of the year.

A party is a good opportunity to meet new people. When you feel like entertaining, you can say you want **dare una festa** *(dah-reh oo-nah feh-stah)* (to give a party). You can also use the expression **fare una festa** *(fah-reh oo-nah feh-stah)* (to make a party).

How do you issue an invitation in Italian? Table 7-1 gives you the first step — the conjugation of the verb **invitare** *(een-vee-tah-reh)* (to invite).

Table 7-1	Conjugating the Verb *Invitare*	
Italian	*Pronunciation*	*Translation*
io invito	ee-oh een-vee-toh	I invite
tu inviti	too een-vee-tee	you (informal, singular) invite
Lei invita	lay een-vee-tah	you (formal, singular) invite
lui/lei invita	loo-ee/lay een-vee-tah	he/she invites
noi invitiamo	noh-ee een-vee-tee-ah-moh	we invite
Voi/voi invitate	voh-ee een-vee-tah-teh	you (formal/informal, plural) invite
loro invitano	loh-roh een-vee-tah-noh	they invite

Suggesting an activity in Italian is not so different from the way you do it in English. You can ask **Perché non** . . . *(pehr-keh nohn)* (Why don't we . . .) or **Che ne pensi** . . . *(keh neh pehn-see)* (What do you think about . . .). The use of "let's," however, is a little different.

In Italian, how you say something and the tone you use differentiates a normal sentence from a suggestion. You say **Andiamo!** *(ahn-dee-ah-moh)* (Let's go!) with enthusiasm and punctuate it with an exclamation point, but **Andiamo al ristorante** *(ahn-dee-ah-moh ahl ree-stoh-rahn-teh)* (We're going to the restaurant) is a normal sentence. The actual form of the verb doesn't change.

If your invitation is accepted, the person might say **Ci sarò** *(chee sah-roh)* (I'll be there).

The word **perché** is special. We use it here to ask the question "why." However, it can also mean "because." A dialogue can go like this:

Perché non mangi? *(pehr-keh nohn mahn-jee)* (Why don't you eat?)

Perché non ho fame. *(pehr-keh nohn oh fah-meh)* (Because I'm not hungry.)

Words to Know

invito [m]	een-vee-toh	invitation
festa [f]	feh-stah	party
ospite [m/f]	oh-spee-teh	host
perché	pehr-keh	why, because
bere	beh-reh	to drink
ballare	bahl-lah-reh	to dance

Getting Out and About

Everybody likes to get away from the daily grind and check out new environments and activities in their free time. Vacationers flock **al mare** *(ahl mah-reh)* (to the beach), head **in montagna** *(een mohn-tah-nyah)* (to the mountains) or **in campagna** *(een kahm-pah-nyah)* (to the country), or take a trip to a **grande città** *(grahn-deh cheet-tah)* (big city) to see the sights.

Maybe you use your **fine settimana** *(fee-neh seht-tee-mah-nah)* (weekends) to play sports like **calcio** *(kahl-choh)* (soccer) or **pallavolo** *(pahl-lah-voh-loh)* (volleyball). Or perhaps you park yourself in front of the TV to watch **pallacanestro** *(pahl-lah-kah-neh-stroh)* (basketball). In any case, being able to talk sports and other recreational activities is a plus in any language.

Enjoying the wonders of nature

Maybe you like to go to the mountains to be close to nature. Even when **ti godi** *(tee goh-dee)* (you enjoy) Mother Nature on your own, you may want to know some vocabulary to express the wonders you see. See Table 7-2.

Table 7-2	Nature	
Italian	*Pronunciation*	*Translation*
verde	vehr-deh	nature
albero [m]	ahl-beh-roh	tree
bosco [m]	boh-skoh	woods
campagna [f]	kahm-pah-nyah	countryside

(continued)

Table 7-2 (continued)

Italian	Pronunciation	Translation
fiore [m]	fee-<u>oh</u>-reh	flower
fiume [m]	fee-<u>oo</u>-meh	river
lago [m]	<u>lah</u>-goh	lake
mare [m]	<u>mah</u>-reh	beach
montagna [f]	mohn-<u>tah</u>-nyah	mountain
pianta [f]	pee-<u>ahn</u>-tah	plant
pino [m]	<u>pee</u>-noh	pine
prato [m]	<u>prah</u>-toh	meadow, lawn
quercia [f]	koo-<u>ehr</u>-chah	oak

While you're out in the country, you might see some **animali** *(ah-nee-<u>mah</u>-lee)* (animals). Table 7-3 gives you the names of some common ones.

Table 7-3	Animals	
Italian	Pronunciation	Translation
cane [m]	<u>kah</u>-neh	dog
cavallo [m]	kah-<u>vahl</u>-loh	horse
gatto [m]	<u>gaht</u>-toh	cat
lupo [m]	<u>loo</u>-poh	wolf
maiale [m]	mah-<u>yah</u>-leh	pig
mucca [f]	<u>mook</u>-kah	cow
pecora [f]	<u>peh</u>-koh-rah	sheep
uccello [m]	ooch-<u>chehl</u>-loh	bird

In a couple of the following sentences related to the outdoors, Italian borrows English words — **picnic** and **jog.**

- ✔ **Mi piace camminare nel verde.** *(mee pee-ah-cheh kahm-mee-nah-reh nehl vehr-deh)* (I like to walk in nature.)

- ✔ **Facciamo un picnic sul prato?** *(fahch-chah-moh oon peek-neek sool prah-toh)* (Should we have a picnic on the lawn?)

- ✔ **Ti piace il osservare gli uccelli?** *(tee pee-ah-cheh eel ohs-sehr-vah-reh lyee ooch-chehl-lee)* (Do you like bird-watching?)

- ✔ **Faccio jogging nel parco.** *(fahch-choh johg-geeng nehl pahr-koh)* (I go jogging in the park.)

- ✔ **Ho una piccola fattoria.** *(oh oo-nah peek-koh-lah faht-toh-ree-ah)* (I have a small farm.)

Taking a tour

Whether you're in a city or a rural area, you can usually find fun and interesting sights. You can take a car trip, or you can leave the driving to someone else and sign up for a guided tour to visit special places. Use the following questions to help find out more about **una gita organizzata** *(oo-nah jee-tah ohr-gah-neet-tsah-tah)* (an organized tour).

Note that Italian has two, basically interchangeable ways to say "go on a tour": **fare una gita** *(fah-reh oo-nah jee-tah)* and **fare un'escursione** *(fah-reh oon-eh-skoor-see-oh-neh).*

Here are some questions you might ask when booking a tour:

- ✔ **Ci sono gite organizzate?** *(chee soh-noh jee-teh ohr-gah-neet-tsah-teh)* (Are there any organized tours?)

- ✔ **Che cosa c'è da vedere?** *(keh koh-zah cheh dah veh-deh-reh)* (What sights are included?)

✔ **Quanto costa la gita?** *(koo-ahn-toh koh-stah lah jee-tah)* (How much does the tour cost?)

✔ **C'è una guida inglese?** *(cheh oo-nah goo-ee-dah een-gleh-zeh)* (Is there an English-speaking guide?)

✔ **Dove si comprano i biglietti?** *(doh-veh see kohm-prah-noh ee bee-lyeht-tee)* (Where do I buy tickets?)

Playing sports

Playing and talking about sports is a favored pastime of people the world over. Some sports you *do* in Italian. You pair those words with the verb **fare** *(fah-reh)* (to do, to practice). Table 7-4 lists the sports that take this verb.

Table 7-4	Sports with the Verb *Fare*	
Italian	*Pronunciation*	*Translation*
atletica	aht-leh-tee-kah	athletics
ciclismo	chee-klee-smoh	cycling
equitazione	eh-koo-ee-tah-dzee-oh-neh	horseback riding
jogging	johg-geeng	jogging
nuoto	noo-oh-toh	swimming
palestra	pah-leh-strah	going to the gym
scherma	skehr-mah	fencing
sci nautico	shee nah-oo-tee-koh	water-skiing

With other sports, you use **giocare** *(joh-kah-reh)* (to play). Table 7-5 lists some popular sports that take this verb.

Table 7-5	Sports with the Verb *Giocare*	
Italian	*Pronunciation*	*Translation*
calcio	<u>kahl</u>-choh	soccer
pallacanestro	pahl-lah-kah-<u>neh</u>-stroh	basketball
pallavolo	pahl-lah-<u>voh</u>-loh	volleyball
tennis	<u>tehn</u>-nees	tennis

Finally, a few sports take the verb **andare** *(ahn-<u>dah</u>-reh)* (to go), including **andare a cavallo** *(ahn-<u>dah</u>-reh ah kah-<u>vahl</u>-loh)* (to ride) and **andare in bicicletta** *(ahn-<u>dah</u>-reh een bee-chee-<u>kleht</u>-tah)* (to cycle).

Table 7-6 gives the conjugations for these three important sports verbs: **fare, andare,** and **giocare.**

Table 7-6	Conjugating the Verbs *Fare, Andare,* and *Giocare*	
Italian	*Pronunciation*	*Translation*
fare	**<u>fah</u>-reh**	**to do**
io faccio	<u>ee</u>-oh <u>fahch</u>-choh	I do
tu fai	too <u>fah</u>-ee	you (informal, singular) do
Lei fa	lay fah	you (formal, singular) do
lui/lei fa	<u>loo</u>-ee/lay fah	he/she does
noi facciamo	<u>noh</u>-ee fahch-<u>chah</u>-moh	we do
Voi/voi fate	<u>voh</u>-ee <u>fah</u>-teh	you (formal/ informal, plural) do
loro fanno	<u>loh</u>-roh <u>fahn</u>-noh	they do

(continued)

Table 7-6 *(continued)*

Italian	Pronunciation	Translation
andare	**ahn-_dah_-reh**	**to go**
io vado	_ee_-oh _vah_-doh	I go
tu vai	too _vah_-ee	you (informal, singular) go
Lei va	lay vah	you (formal, singular) go
lui/lei va	_loo_-ee/lay vah	he/she goes
noi andiamo	_noh_-ee ahn-dee-_ah_-moh	we go
Voi/voi andate	_voh_-ee ahn-_dah_-teh	you (formal/informal, plural) go
loro vanno	_loh_-roh _vahn_-noh	they go
giocare	**joh-_kah_-reh**	**to play**
io gioco	_ee_-oh _joh_-koh	I play
tu giochi	too _joh_-kee	you (informal, singular) play
Lei gioca	lay _joh_-kah	you (formal, singular) play
lui/lei gioca	_loo_-ee/lay _joh_-kah	he/she plays
noi giochiamo	_noh_-ee joh-kee-_ah_-moh	we play
Voi/voi giocate	_voh_-ee joh-_kah_-teh	you (formal/informal, plural) play
loro giocano	_loh_-roh _joh_-kah-noh	they play

You can follow sports ranging from tennis to **pugilato** *(poo-jee-_lah_-toh)* (boxing) to **Formula 1** *(_fohr_-moo-lah oo-noh)* (Formula One car racing). Or you can be a bit more active and participate in sports like these:

✔ **camminare** *(kahm-mee-nah-reh)* (hiking)

✔ **fare equitazione** *(fah-reh eh-koo-ee-tah-dzee-oh-neh)* (horseback riding)

✔ **fare snowboarding** *(fah-reh snoo-bohr-ding)* (snowboarding)

✔ **fare vela** *(fah-reh veh-lah)* (sailing)

✔ **pattinare** *(paht-tee-nah-reh)* (ice skating)

✔ **pescare** *(peh-skah-reh)* (fishing)

✔ **sciare** *(shee-ah-reh)* (skiing)

In Italy, the most popular sports are **il calcio** *(eel kahl-choh)* (soccer) and **il ciclismo** *(eel chee-klee-smoh)* (cycling). Just think of the worldwide event known as **Giro d'Italia** *(jee-roh dee-tah-lee-ah),* the Italian bicycling tour.

Chapter 8

When You Gotta Work

. . . .

In This Chapter

▶ Talking about business

▶ Having a phone conversation

▶ Making appointments

▶ Leaving a message

. . . .

*B*usiness contact with people in other countries continually increases in importance. Because modern technology supports the quick exchange of information over long distances, you may have to talk to foreign business partners or even travel to their countries. If you happen to have contact with an Italian company or businessperson, knowing some basic Italian business vocabulary is useful. English is the language of business, though, and Italian has adopted many English computer terms.

Talking Shop

Italian has at least three words for "company," and they're interchangeable:

▶ **la compagnia** (*lah kohm-pah-nyee-ah*)

▶ **la ditta** (*lah deet-tah*) (which also means "the firm")

▶ **la società** (*lah soh-cheh-tah*)

L'ufficio *(loof-fee-choh)* means "office," but people often use **stanza** *(stahn-tsah)* (room) to refer to their personal office.

Talking about work is hard to do without the verb **lavorare** *(lah-voh-rah-reh)* (to work). Table 8-1 gives the conjugation of this hard-working verb.

Table 8-1	Conjugating the Verb *Lavorare*	
Italian	**Pronunciation**	**Translation**
io lavoro	ee-oh lah-voh-roh	I work
tu lavori	too lah-voh-ree	you (informal, singular) work
Lei lavora	lay lah-voh-rah	you (formal, singular) work
lui/lei lavora	loo-ee/lay lah-voh-rah	he/she works
noi lavoriamo	noh-ee lah-voh-ree-ah-moh	we work
Voi/voi lavorate	voh-ee lah-voh-rah-teh	you (formal/ informal, plural) work
loro lavorano	loh-roh lah-voh-rah-noh	they work

Common professions

Il lavoro *(eel lah-voh-roh)* (job, work) is a popular topic for small talk. Table 8-2 lists the Italian words for common professions.

Table 8-2	Professions	
Italian	**Pronunciation**	**Translation**
architetto [f/m]	ahr-kee-teht-toh	architect
avvocato [f/m]	ahv-voh-kah-toh	lawyer

Italian	Pronunciation	Translation
commessa [f]/ commesso [m]	kohm-<u>mehs</u>-sah/ kohm-<u>mehs</u>-soh	clerk
giornalista [f/m]	johr-nah-<u>lee</u>-stah	journalist
ingegnere [f/m]	een-jeh-<u>nyeh</u>-reh	engineer
insegnante [f/m]	een-seh-<u>nyahn</u>-teh	teacher
meccanico [f/m]	mehk-<u>kah</u>-nee-koh	mechanic
medico [f/m]	<u>meh</u>-dee-koh	doctor
regista [f/m]	reh-<u>jee</u>-stah	film director

When you talk about your profession in Italian, you don't need to use the article *a,* as in "I'm a doctor." You simply say **sono medico** *(<u>soh</u>-noh <u>meh</u>-dee-koh).*

The human element

Even if you're a **libero professionista** *(<u>lee</u>-beh-roh proh-fehs-see-oh-<u>nee</u>-stah)* (self-employed person), chances are that your job puts you in contact with other people. All those people have titles, as the following short exchanges show:

✔ **Il mio capo è una donna.** *(eel <u>mee</u>-oh <u>kah</u>-poh eh <u>oo</u>-nah <u>dohn</u>-nah)* (My boss is a woman.)

  Il mio è un tiranno! *(eel <u>mee</u>-oh eh oon tee-<u>rahn</u>-noh)* (Mine is bossy!)

✔ **Hai un assistente/un'assistente personale?** *(<u>ah</u>-ee oon ahs-see-<u>stehn</u>-teh/oon-ahs-see-<u>stehn</u>-teh pehr-soh-<u>nah</u>-leh)* (Do you have a personal assistant?)

  No, il nostro team ha un segretario/una segretaria. *(noh eel <u>noh</u>-stroh teem ah oon seh-greh-<u>tah</u>-ree-oh/<u>oo</u>-nah seh-greh-<u>tah</u>-ree-ah)* (No, our team has a secretary.)

✔ **Dov'è il direttore?** *(doh-<u>veh</u> eel dee-reht-<u>toh</u>-reh)* (Where is the manager/boss?)

Nel suo stanza./Nella sua stanza. *(nehl <u>soo</u>-oh <u>stahn</u>-tsah/<u>nehl</u>-lah <u>soo</u>-ah <u>stahn</u>-tsah)* (In his office./In her office.)

Words to Know

colleghi [m]	kohl-<u>leh</u>-gee	colleagues
superiori [m]	soo-peh-ree-<u>oh</u>-ree	supervisors
capo [m]	<u>kah</u>-poh	boss
segretario [m]	seh-greh-<u>tah</u>-ree-oh	secretary
domanda d'assunzione [f]	doh-<u>mahn</u>-dah dahs-soon-tsee-<u>oh</u>-neh	job application
colloquio [m]	kohl-<u>loh</u>-koo-ee-oh	interview
biglietto da visita [m]	bee-<u>lyeht</u>-toh dah <u>vee</u>-see-tah	business card

Office equipment

Even the smallest offices utilize a variety of equipment. Fortunately, many technology-related words are the same in Italian as they are in English. For example, computer, fax, and e-mail are used and pronounced as they are in English, and the Italian for "photocopy" and "photocopier" are fairly intuitive — **fotocopia** *(foh-toh-koh-pee-ah)* and **fotocopiatrice** *(foh-toh-koh-pee-ah-tree-cheh),* respectively.

Here's some additional office-equipment vocabulary:

- ✔ **la stampante** *(lah stahm-pahn-teh)* (the printer)
- ✔ **il fax** *(eel fahks)* (the fax)
- ✔ **la macchina** *(lah mahk-kee-nah)* (the machine)
- ✔ **l'e-mail** *(lee-mail)* (the e-mail)
- ✔ **un indirizzo e-mail** *(oon een-dee-reet-tsoh ee-mail)* (an e-mail address)
- ✔ **il messaggio** *(eel mehs-sahj-joh)* (the message)
- ✔ **Non funziona, è rotto.** *(nohn foon-dzee-oh-nah eh roht-toh)* (It's not working; It's out of order.)

Chatting on the Phone

Pronto! *(prohn-toh)* (Hello!) is the first thing you hear when you talk to an Italian on the telephone. This word is special, though: In most languages, you answer the phone with the same word you use for hello in any setting, but in Italian, you use **pronto** to say hello only on the phone.

Pronto means more than just hello. It frequently means "ready," in which case it functions as an adjective and therefore changes according to the noun it modifies. If the noun it modifies is masculine, the adjective ends in *-o,* as in **pronto.** If the noun is feminine, it ends in *-a,* as in **pronta** *(prohn-tah).* Consider these examples:

- ✔ **Martino, sei pronto?** *(mahr-tee-noh say prohn-toh)* (Martino, are you ready?)
- ✔ **La cena è pronta.** *(lah cheh-nah eh prohn-tah)* (Dinner is ready.)

Another use of **pronto** that you should know is **pronto soccorso** (*prohn-toh sohk-kohr-soh*) (first aid, emergency room). In this context, **pronto** means "rapid."

Italians are fanatical about cellphones. Finding an Italian who doesn't own a cellphone, which they call **il cellulare** (*eel chehl-loo-lah-reh*), is a tough task. They love these gadgets so much that they've given them an affectionate nickname — **il telefonino** (*eel teh-leh-foh-nee-noh*), which literally means "little phone."

If you're the one making the call, you respond to **pronto** by identifying yourself:

> ✔ **Sono Giorgio.** (*soh-noh johr-joh*) (It's Giorgio.)
>
> ✔ **Sono io!** (*soh-noh ee-oh*) (It's me!)
>
> ✔ **Con chì parlo?** (*kohn kee pahr-loh*) (Who am I speaking to?)

The person on the other end of the line, especially in a business situation, might say **Mi dica!** (*mee dee-kah*) [Can I help you? (literally, Tell me!)]

Calling from a public phone

We have to tell you something about **il telefono pubblico** (*eel teh-leh-foh-noh poob-blee-koh*) (the public phone). If you don't have a cellphone and you need to call someone while you're out and about, you look for **una cabina telefonica** (*oo-nah kah-bee-nah teh-leh-foh-nee-kah*) (a phone booth). These phones are either **un telefono a monete** (*oon teh-leh-foh-noh ah moh-neh-teh*) (a coin-operated phone) or **un telefono a scheda** (*oon teh-leh-foh-noh ah skeh-dah*) (a card phone).

In Italy, a phone card is called either **la carta telefonica** (*lah kahr-tah teh-leh-foh-nee-kah*) or **la scheda telefonica** (*lah skeh-dah teh-leh-foh-nee-kah*). You can get one at **tabaccai** (*tah-bahk-kah-ee*) (kiosks selling tobacco, newspapers, and so on) or at the post office.

Here are some helpful pay-phone phrases:

- ✔ **C'è/Avete un telefono?** *(cheh-ah-veh-teh oon teh-leh-foh-noh)* [Is there/Do you have a (public) telephone?]

- ✔ **È a monete?** *(eh ah moh-neh-teh)* (Is it coin-operated?)

- ✔ **Avete schede telefoniche?** *(ah-veh-teh skeh-deh teh-leh-foh-nee-keh)* (Do you sell phone cards?)

- ✔ **Il telefono dà libero.** *(eel teh-leh-foh-noh dah lee-beh-roh)* (The line is free.)

- ✔ **Il telefono dà occupato.** *(eel teh-leh-foh-noh dah ohk-koo-pah-toh)* (The line is busy.)

- ✔ **Il telefono squilla.** *(eel teh-leh-foh-noh skoo-eel-lah)* (The telephone is ringing.)

- ✔ **Rispondi!** *(ree-spohn-dee)* (Answer!; Pick up the phone!)

- ✔ **Attacca!** *(aht-tahk-kah)* (Hang up!)

If you don't know a **numero di telefono** *(noo-meh-roh dee teh-leh-foh-noh)* (telephone number), you have three ways to get it:

- ✔ Look it up in the **elenco telefonico** *(eh-lehn-koh teh-leh-foh-nee-koh)* (phone book).

- ✔ If it's a business number, look in the **pagine gialle** *(pah-jee-neh jahl-leh)* (yellow pages).

- ✔ Call the **servizio informazioni** *(sehr-vee-dzee-oh een-fohr-mah-dzee-oh-nee)* (directory information).

Calling for business or pleasure

Whether you want to make an appointment, find out what time a show starts, or just chat with a friend, the easiest way is usually to pick up the phone. Table 8-3 shows you the conjugations of the verbs **parlare** *(pahr-lah-reh)* (to speak) and **chiamare** *(kee-ah-mah-reh)* (to call).

Table 8-3	Conjugating the Verbs *Parlare* and *Chiamare*	
Italian	*Pronunciation*	*Translation*
parlare	**pahr-lah-reh**	**to speak**
io parlo	ee-oh pahr-loh	I speak
tu parli	too pahr-lee	you (informal, singular) speak
Lei parla	lay pahr-lah	you (formal, singular) speak
lui/lei parla	loo-ee/lay pahr-lah	he/she speaks
noi parliamo	noh-ee pahr-lee-ah-moh	we speak
Voi/voi parlate	voh-ee pahr-lah-teh	you (formal/ informal, plural) speak
loro parlano	loh-roh pahr-lah-noh	they speak
chiamare	**kee-ah-mah-reh**	**to call**
io chiamo	ee-oh kee-ah-moh	I call
tu chiami	too kee-ah-mee	you (informal, singular) call
Lei chiama	lay kee-ah-mah	you (formal, singular) call
lui/lei chiama	loo-ee/lay kee-ah-mah	he/she calls
noi chiamiamo	noh-ee kee-ah-mee-ah-moh	we call
Voi/voi chiamate	voh-ee kee-ah-mah-teh	you (formal/ informal, plural) call
loro chiamano	loh-roh kee-ah-mah-noh	they call

Sometimes you call just to chat — **fare due chiacchiere al telefono** (*fah-reh doo-eh kee-ahk-kee-eh-reh ahl teh-leh-foh-noh*). But the person on the other end of the line may not be prepared for it. So you may want to ask (or you may hear that person say):

> ✔ **Sei occupata?** (*say ohk-koo-pah-tah*) (Are you busy?)
>
> ✔ **Ti posso richiamare?** (*tee pohs-soh ree-kee-ah-mah-reh*) (Can I call you back?)

Words to Know

cellulare; telefonino [m]	chehl-loo-lah-reh; teh-leh-foh-nee-noh	cellphone
cabina telefonica [f]	kah-bee-nah teh-leh-foh-nee-kah	telephone booth
telefono pubblico [m]	teh-leh-foh-noh poob-blee-koh	public phone
telefono a monete [m]	teh-leh-foh-noh ah moh-neh-teh	coin-operated phone
carta/scheda telefonica [f]	kahr-tah/skeh-dah teh-leh-foh-nee-kah	phone card

Asking for People and Leaving a Message

You often use the phone to get in touch with someone for business or pleasure, so it's good to know how to ask for the person you want. In case the person you want isn't available, you need to be comfortable getting a message across.

The following exchange gives you some useful phrases for using the telephone:

Buongiorno, sono Leo. C'è Camilla? *(boo-ohn-johr-noh soh-noh leh-oh cheh kah-meel-lah)* (Good morning, this is Leo. Is Camilla in?)

No, è appena uscita. *(noh eh ahp-peh-nah oo-shee-tah)* (No, she's just gone out.)

Quando la trovo? *(koo-ahn-doh lah troh-voh)* (When can I reach her?)

Verso le nove. *(vehr-soh leh noh-veh)* (Around nine.)

Le posso lasciare un messaggio? *(leh pohs-soh lah-shah-reh oon mehs-sahj-joh)* (Can I leave her a message?)

Here's a short dialogue that's more typical of a business situation:

Buongiorno, dica. *(boo-ohn-johr-noh dee-kah)* (Good morning, can I help you?)

Potrei parlare con il signor Trevi? *(poh-tray pahr-lah-reh kohn eel see-nyohr treh-vee)* (May I speak to Mr. Trevi?)

Mi dispiace, è in riunione. *(mee dee-spee-ah-cheh eh een ree-oon-yoh-neh)* (I'm sorry, he's in a meeting.)

Potrei lasciargli un messaggio? *(poh-tray lah-shahr-lyee oon mehs-sahj-joh)* (Can I leave him a message?)

Perhaps you want to check for messages. You're familiar with the situation: You're waiting for a call, but the phone doesn't ring. Then you have to go out. When you get back, you want to know whether anyone called for you. You can ask that question in several ways:

✔ **Ha chiamato qualcuno per me?** *(ah kee-ah-mah-toh koo-ahl-koo-noh pehr meh)* (Has anybody called for me?)

✔ **Mi ha chiamato qualcuno?** *(mee ah kee-ah-<u>mah</u>-toh koo-ahl-<u>koo</u>-noh)* (Did anybody call me?)

✔ **Chi ha telefonato?** *(kee ah teh-leh-foh-<u>nah</u>-toh)* (Who called?)

✔ **Chiamate per me?** *(kee-ah-<u>mah</u>-teh pehr meh)* (Are there any calls for me?)

Words to Know

pronto	<u>prohn</u>-toh	hello
arrivederci	ahr-ree-veh-<u>dehr</u>-chee	good-bye
chiacchierare	kee-ahk-kee-eh-<u>rah</u>-reh	to chat
Attenda in linea!	aht-<u>tehn</u>-dah een <u>lee</u>-neh-ah	Hold the line!
chiamare	kee-ah-<u>mah</u>-reh	to call
chiamata [f]	kee-ah-<u>mah</u>-tah	call
informazione [f]	een-fohr-mah-dzee-<u>oh</u>-neh	information

Chapter 9

I Get Around: Transportation

In This Chapter

▶ Traveling by airplane

▶ Declaring goods to customs

▶ Renting a car and using public transportation

▶ Asking for directions

*W*hether you're visiting Italy or you just need to explain to an Italian-speaking friend how to get across town, transportation vocab really comes in handy. This chapter helps you make your way through an airport and get through customs and helps you secure transportation when you're on the ground, either by taxi, bus, car, or train. Finally, we show you how to rent a car and how to ask for directions (but we *don't* tell you how to make someone *else* ask for directions!).

Getting through the Airport

At an Italian airport, you can likely get by with English, but the person you encounter may know only Italian. Just in case, you need to know some useful words and phrases. Besides, you'll probably want to practice the language in which you'll be immersed when you step outside the airport.

Checking in

The moment you finally get rid of your luggage is called check-in — or, in Italian, **accettazione** *(ahch-cheht-tah-tsee-oh-neh)*. You also pick up your **carta d'imbarco** *(kahr-tah deem-bahr-koh)* (boarding pass) at the check-in counter.

Here are some things the ticket agent might say to you:

- ✔ **Il Suo biglietto, per favore.** *(eel soo-oh bee-lyeht-toh pehr fah-voh-reh)* (Your ticket, please.)

- ✔ **Passaporto?** *(pahs-sah-pohr-toh)* (Passport?)

- ✔ **Quanti bagagli ha?** *(koo-ahn-tee bah-gah-lyee ah)* (How many suitcases do you have?)

- ✔ **Preferisce un posto vicino al finestrino o al corridoio?** *(preh-feh-ree-sheh oon poh-stoh vee-chee-noh ahl fee-neh-stree-noh oh ahl kohr-ree-doh-ee-oh)* (Do you prefer a window or an aisle seat?)

- ✔ **L'imbarco è alle nove e quindici, uscita tre.** *(leem-bahr-koh eh ahl-leh noh-veh eh koo-een-dee-chee oo-shee-tah treh)* (Boarding is at 9:15, gate 3.)

Words to Know

passaporto [m]	pahs-sah-pohr-toh	passport
valigia [f]	vah-lee-jah	suitcase
borsa [f] a mano	bohr-sah ah mah-noh	carry-on bag
bagaglio [m]	bah-gah-lyoh	baggage
arrivo [m]	ahr-ree-voh	arrival
partenza [f]	pahr-tehn-dzah	departure

| destinazione [f] | deh-stee-nah-tsee-<u>oh</u>-neh | destination |
| uscita [f] | oo-<u>shee</u>-tah | gate |

Waiting to board the plane

Before boarding, you may encounter unforeseen situations, such as delays. If you do, you'll probably want to ask some questions. The following sentences represent a typical conversation about this topic:

> ✔ **Il volo è in orario?** *(eel <u>voh</u>-loh eh een oh-<u>rah</u>-ree-oh)* (Is the flight on time?)

> ✔ **No, è in ritardo.** *(noh eh een ree-<u>tahr</u>-doh)* (No, there has been a delay.)

> ✔ **Di quanto?** *(dee koo-<u>ahn</u>-toh)* (How much?)

> ✔ **Circa quindici minuti.** *(<u>cheer</u>-kah koo-<u>een</u>-dee-chee mee-<u>noo</u>-tee)* (About 15 minutes.)

While you're waiting, two other questions may come in handy:

> ✔ **Dov'è il bar?** *(doh-<u>veh</u> eel bahr)* (Where is the bar?)

> ✔ **Dove sono i servizi?** *(<u>doh</u>-veh <u>soh</u>-noh ee sehr-<u>vee</u>-dzee)* (Where are the bathrooms?)

Words to Know

volo [m]	<u>voh</u>-loh	flight
in ritardo	een ree-<u>tahr</u>-doh	late, delayed
in orario	een oh-rah-<u>ree</u>-oh	on time
servizi [m]	sehr-<u>vee</u>-dzee	the bathrooms

Taking care of business after landing

After your plane lands, you have to take care of necessities, such as finding a bathroom, changing money, looking for the baggage claim area, and securing a luggage cart and a taxi. The following questions may come in handy:

- ✔ **Dov'è un bancomat?** *(doh-veh oon bahn-koh-maht)* (Where is an ATM?)

- ✔ **C'è anche una banca?** *(cheh ahn-keh oo-nah bahn-kah)* (Is there also a bank?)

- ✔ **Dove sono i carrelli?** *(doh-veh soh-noh ee kahr-rehl-lee)* (Where are the luggage carts?)

See Chapter 3 for more on changing money.

Words to Know		
in vacanza	een vah-kahn-dzah	on vacation
per lavoro	pehr lah-voh-roh	on business
consegna bagagli [f]	kohn-seh-nyah bah-gah-lyee	baggage claim
cambio [m]	kahm-bee-oh	money exchange
entrata [f]	ehn-trah-tah	entrance
uscita [f]	oo-shee-tah	exit

Going through customs

You can't get into a foreign country without going through **dogana** *(doh-gah-nah)* (customs). The customs agent asks **Niente da dichiarare?** *(nee-ehn-teh dah dee-kee-ah-rah-reh)* (Anything to declare?) You respond in one of two ways:

✔ If you have something to declare, say **Ho questo/queste cose da dichiarare.** *(oh koo-eh-stoh/koo-eh-steh koh-zeh dah dee-kee-ah-rah-reh)* (I have to declare this/these things.)

✔ If not, say **No, niente.** *(noh nee-ehn-teh)* (No, nothing.)

In some cases, the customs agent will say **Per questo deve pagare il dazio.** *(pehr koo-eh-stoh deh-veh pah-gah-reh eel dah-dzee-oh)* (You have to pay duty on this.)

Words to Know

controllo passaporti [m]	kohn-trohl-loh pahs-sah-pohr-tee	passport control
dogana [f]	doh-gah-nah	customs
dichiarare	dee-kee-ah-rah-reh	to declare
niente [m]	nee-ehn-teh	nothing
pagare	pah-gah-reh	to pay

Renting a Car

If you don't have a car, you may need to rent one when you go on vacation. Whether you rent a car by phone or from a rental agency, the process is the same: Just tell the rental company what kind of car you want and under what conditions you want to rent it. The following dialogue represents a typical conversation with a rental agent:

Vorrei noleggiare una macchina. *(vohr-ray noh-lehj-jah-reh oo-nah mahk-kee-nah)* (I would like to rent a car.)

Che tipo? *(keh tee-poh)* (What kind?)

Di media cilindrata col cambio automatico.
(dee meh-dee-ah chee-leen-drah-tah kohl kahm-bee-oh ah-oo-toh-mah-tee-koh) (A midsize with an automatic transmission.)

Per quanto tempo? *(pehr koo-ahn-toh tehm-poh)* (For how long?)

Una settimana. *(oo-nah seht-tee-mah-nah)* (One week.)

Quanto costa a settimana? *(koo-ahn-toh koh-stah ah seht-tee-mah-nah)* (What does it cost for a week?)

C'è una tariffa speciale. *(cheh oo-nah tah-reef-fah speh-chah-leh)* (There is a special rate.)

L'assicurazione è inclusa? *(lahs-see-koo-rah-dzee-oh-neh eh een-kloo-zah)* (Is insurance included?)

Sì, con la polizza casco. *(see kohn lah poh-leet-tsah kah-skoh)* (Yes, a comprehensive policy.)

Table 9-1 lists some other expressions you may need when renting a car or getting gas.

Table 9-1   Car-Related Terms and Phrases

Italian	Pronunciation	Translation
l'aria condizionata [f]	lah-ree-ah kohn-dee-dzee-oh-nah-tah	air conditioning
il cabriolet [m]	eel kah-bree-oh-leh	convertible
fare benzina	fah-reh behn-dzee-nah	to put in gas
Faccia il pieno.	fahch-chah eel pee-eh-noh	Fill it up.
la benzina senza piombo [f]	lah behn-dzee-nah sehn-tsah pee-ohm-boh	unleaded fuel

Italian	Pronunciation	Translation
la benzina super [f]	lah behn-<u>dzee</u>-nah <u>soo</u>-pehr	premium fuel
Controlli l'olio.	kohn-<u>trohl</u>-lee <u>loh</u>-lee-oh	Check the oil.

Navigating Public Transportation

If you'd rather not drive yourself, you can get around quite comfortably by using taxis, trains, and buses. This section tells you how to do so in Italian.

Taking a taxi

The process of hailing a taxi is the same in Italy as it is in the United States. You even use the same word: **taxi** *(<u>tah</u>-ksee)*. Here are two phrases to use when requesting help getting a cab:

> ✔ **Può chiamarmi un taxi?** *(poo-<u>oh</u> kee-ah-<u>mahr</u>-mee oon <u>tah</u>-ksee)* (Can you call me a taxi?)

> ✔ **Vorrei un taxi, per favore.** *(vohr-<u>ray</u> oon <u>tah</u>-ksee pehr fah-<u>voh</u>-reh)* (I'd like a taxi, please.)

In case you're asked **per quando?** *(pehr koo-<u>ahn</u>-doh)* (when?), you need to be prepared with an answer. Here are some possibilities:

> ✔ **subito** *(<u>soo</u>-bee-toh)* (right now)

> ✔ **fra un'ora** *(frah oon-<u>oh</u>-rah)* (in one hour)

> ✔ **alle due del pomeriggio** *(<u>ahl</u>-leh <u>doo</u>-eh dehl poh-meh-<u>reej</u>-joh)* (at 2:00 p.m.)

> ✔ **domani mattina** *(doh-<u>mah</u>-nee maht-<u>tee</u>-nah)* (tomorrow morning)

After you seat yourself in a taxi, the driver will ask where you want to go. Here are some potential destinations:

✔ **Alla stazione, per favore.** *(ahl-lah stah-dzee-oh-neh pehr fah-voh-reh)* (To the station, please.)

✔ **All'areoporto.** *(ahl-lah-reh-oh-pohr-toh)* (To the airport.)

✔ **A questo indirizzo: via Leopardi, numero 3.** *(ah koo-eh-stoh een-dee-reet-tsoh vee-ah leh-oh-pahr-dee noo-meh-roh treh)* (To this address: via Leopardi, number 3.)

Finally, you have to pay. Simply ask the driver **Quant'è?** *(koo-ahn-teh)* (How much?). For more info about money, see Chapter 3.

Getting around by train

You can buy a train ticket **alla stazione** *(ahl-lah stah-dzee-oh-neh)* (at the station) or at **un'agenzia di viaggi** *(oo-nah-jehn-dzee-ah dee vee-ahj-jee)* (a travel agency). If you want to take a **treno rapido** *(treh-noh rah-pee-doh)* (express train), you pay a **supplemento** *(soop-pleh-mehn-toh)* (surcharge). These faster trains in Italy are called Inter City (IC) — or Euro City (EC) if their final destination is outside Italy.

Following are some words and phrases that can help you purchase the right ticket:

✔ **treni diretti** *(treh-nee dee-reht-tee)* (direct trains)

✔ **un locale** *(oon loh-kah-leh)* (a slow train)

✔ **in prima classe** *(een pree-mah klahs-seh)* (first class)

✔ **in seconda classe** *(een seh-kohn-dah klahs-seh)* (second class)

✔ **andata e ritorno** *(ahn-dah-tah eh ree-tohr-noh)* (round-trip)

✔ **solo andata** *(soh-loh ahn-dah-tah)* (one-way)

✔ **Devo cambiare?** *(deh-voh kahm-bee-ah-reh)* (Do I have to change [trains]?)

✔ **la coincidenza** *(lah koh-een-chee-dehn-dzah)* (the connection)

✔ **A che ora parte il prossimo treno?** *(ah keh oh-rah pahr-teh eel prohs-see-moh treh-noh)* (What time is the next train?)

✔ **Un biglietto per Perugia, per favore.** *(oon bee-lyeht-toh pehr peh-roo-jah pehr fah-voh-reh)* (One ticket to Perugia, please.)

✔ **il binario** *(eel bee-nah-ree-oh)* (the platform, track)

✔ **Da che binario parte?** *(dah keh bee-nah-ree-oh pahr-teh)* (From which track does it leave?)

✔ **Dal tre.** *(dahl treh)* (From [track number] 3.)

Going by bus or tram

To get from point A to point B without a car, you can take a bus or a tram. This section provides the appropriate Italian vocabulary for such situations.

Some Italian cities have streetcars, or trams, and most have buses. In Italian, they spell it **il tram** *(eel trahm)*. The general Italian word for bus is **l'autobus** *(lah-oo-toh-boos)*. Little buses are called **il pullmino** *(eel pool-mee-noh),* and big buses that take you from one city to another are called **il pullman** *(eel pool-mahn)* or **la corriera** *(lah kohr-ree-eh-rah).*

You can buy bus or tram tickets in bars, **dal giornalaio** *(dahl johr-nah-lah-ee-oh)* (at newspaper stands), or **dal tabaccaio** *(dahl tah-bahk-kah-ee-oh)* (at a tobacco shop).

Italian tobacco shops are little shops where you can purchase cigarettes, stamps, newspapers, and so on. You find them on virtually every street corner in Italy; they're recognizable by either a black-and-white sign or a blue-and-white sign with a big T on it.

Reading the schedules can be difficult for travelers because they're usually written only in Italian. You frequently find the following words on schedules:

- **l'orario** (loh-*rah*-ree-oh) (the timetable)

- **partenze** (pahr-*tehn*-dzeh) (departures)

- **arrivi** (ahr-*ree*-vee) (arrivals)

- **giorni feriali** (*johr*-nee feh-ree-*ah*-lee) (weekdays)

- **giorni festivi** (*johr*-nee feh-*stee*-vee) (Sundays and holidays)

- **il binario** (eel bee-*nah*-ree-oh) (the track, platform)

Words to Know

Scusi, che autobus va . . . ?	*skoo*-zee keh *ah*-oo-toh-boos vah	Excuse me, which bus goes . . . ?
metropolitana [f]	meh-troh-poh-lee-*tah*-nah	subway
fermata della metropolitana [f]	fehr-*mah*-tah *dehl*-lah meh-troh-poh-lee-*tah*-nah	subway station
la prossima fermata [f]	lah *pros*-see-mah fehr-*mah*-tah	the next stop

Asking for Directions

Have you ever been lost in a foreign place? If so, you realize how helpful it is to know enough of the native language to be able to ask for directions. Knowing the language also enables you to understand the answer. In this section, we give you some conversational tips that make it easier to find your way around.

Asking for specific places

When asking for directions, it's always polite to begin with one of the following expressions:

- ✔ **Mi scusi.** *(mee skoo-zee)* (Excuse me.)

- ✔ **Scusi.** *(skoo-zee)* (Excuse me.)

- ✔ **Per favore.** *(pehr fah-voh-reh)* (Please.)

Then you can continue with your question, like the following:

- ✔ **Dov'è il Colosseo?** *(doh-veh el koh-lohs-seh-oh)* (Where is the Colosseum?)

- ✔ **Questa è via Garibaldi?** *(koo-eh-stah eh vee-ah gah-ree-bahl-dee)* (Is this Garibaldi Street?)

- ✔ **Come si arriva alla stazione?** *(koh-meh see ahr-ree-vah ahl-lah stah-dzee-oh-neh)* (How do I get to the station?)

- ✔ **Può indicarmi la strada per il centro?** *(poo-oh een-dee-kahr-mee lah strah-dah pehr eel chehn-troh)* (Can you show me the way downtown?)

- ✔ **Dove siamo adesso?** *(doh-veh see-ah-moh ah-dehs-soh)* (Where are we now?)

- ✔ **Mi sono perso. Dov'è il duomo?** *(mee soh-noh pehr-soh doh-veh eel doo-oh-moh)* (I've lost my way. Where is the cathedral?)

Here are some possible answers to these questions:

- ✔ **Segua la strada principale fino al centro.** *(seh-goo-ah lah strah-dah preen-chee-pah-leh fee-noh ahl chehn-troh)* (Follow the main street to the center of the city.)

- ✔ **Vada sempre dritto.** *(vah-dah sehm-preh dreet-toh)* (Go straight ahead.)

- **Dopo il semaforo giri a destra.** *(doh-poh eel seh-mah-foh-roh jee-ree ah deh-strah)* (After the traffic light, turn right.)
- **È in fondo a sinistra.** *(eh een fohn-doh ah see-nee-strah)* (It's at the end, on the left side.)
- **È vicino alla posta.** *(eh vee-chee-noh ahl-lah poh-stah)* (It's next to the post office.)
- **Attraversi il ponte, poi c'è una piazza e lì lo vede.** *(aht-trah-vehr-see eel pohn-teh poh-ee cheh oo-nah pee-aht-tsah eh lee loh veh-deh)* (Cross the bridge, then there's a square and there you see it.)

Getting oriented

Four orientations are the cardinal points of the compass:

- **nord** *(nohrd)* (north)
- **est** *(ehst)* (east)
- **sud** *(sood)* (south)
- **ovest** *(oh-vehst)* (west)

You may hear the directions used in sentences like these:

- **Trieste è a nord-est.** *(tree-eh-steh eh ah nohrd-ehst)* (Trieste is in the northeast.)
- **Napoli è a sud.** *(nah-poh-lee eh ah sood)* (Naples is in the south.)
- **Roma è a ovest.** *(roh-mah eh ah oh-vehst)* (Rome is in the west.)
- **Bari è a sud-est.** *(bah-ree eh ah sood-ehst)* (Bari is in the southeast.)

You need to know how to orient yourself in relation to people and buildings when following or giving directions. Following are some useful terms that describe spatial relationships:

- ✔ **davanti a** *(dah-vahn-tee ah)* (in front of, opposite)

- ✔ **di fronte a** *(dee frohn-teh ah)* (opposite, in front of)

  In almost all cases, these terms are interchangeable.

- ✔ **dietro a** *(dee-eh-troh ah)* (behind)

- ✔ **vicino a** *(vee-chee-noh ah)* (beside, next to)

- ✔ **dentro** *(dehn-troh)* (inside)

- ✔ **fuori** *(foo-oh-ree)* (outside)

- ✔ **sotto** *(soht-toh)* (under, below)

- ✔ **sopra** *(soh-prah)* (above)

You also need to know relationships between distance and **la direzione** *(lah dee-reh-tsee-oh-neh)* (the direction):

- ✔ **dritto** *(dreet-toh)* (straight)

- ✔ **sempre dritto** *(sehm-preh dreet-toh)* (straight ahead)

- ✔ **fino a** *(fee-noh ah)* (to, up to, until)

- ✔ **prima** *(pree-mah)* (before)

- ✔ **dopo** *(doh-poh)* (after)

- ✔ **a destra** *(ah deh-strah)* (on the right)

- ✔ **a sinistra** *(ah see-nee-strah)* (on the left)

- ✔ **dietro l'angolo** *(dee-eh-troh lahn-goh-loh)* (around the corner)

- ✔ **all'angolo** *(ahl-lahn-goh-loh)* (at the corner)

- ✔ **all'incrocio** *(ahl-leen-kroh-choh)* (at the intersection)

Here's some more vocab for giving and receiving directions:

- ✔ **il marciapiede** *(eel mahr-chah-pee-eh-deh)* (sidewalk)

- ✔ **la piazza** *(lah pee-aht-tsah)* (square)

- ✔ **il ponte** *(eel <u>pohn</u>-teh)* (bridge)
- ✔ **il sottopassaggio** *(eel soht-toh-pahs-<u>sahj</u>-joh)* (underpass)
- ✔ **la strada** *(lah <u>strah</u>-dah)* (road, street)
- ✔ **la via** *(lah <u>vee</u>-ah)* (road, street)
- ✔ **la via principale** *(lah <u>vee</u>-ah preen-chee-<u>pah</u>-leh)* (main street)
- ✔ **il viale** *(eel vee-<u>ah</u>-leh)* (parkway, avenue)
- ✔ **il vicolo** *(eel <u>vee</u>-koh-loh)* (alley, lane)

La strada and **la via** are synonymous, but you always use **via** when the name is specified:

- ✔ **E' una strada molto lunga.** *(eh <u>oo</u>-nah <u>strah</u>-dah <u>mohl</u>-toh <u>loon</u>-gah)* (It's a very long road.)
- ✔ **Abito in via Merulana.** *(<u>ah</u>-bee-toh een <u>vee</u>-ah meh-roo-<u>lah</u>-nah)* (I live on Merulana Street.)

What to say when you don't understand

If you don't understand the directions someone gives you, you need to ask that person to repeat the directions. Here are some useful expressions:

- ✔ **Come, scusi?** *(<u>koh</u>-meh <u>skoo</u>-zee)* (I beg your pardon?)
- ✔ **Mi scusi, non ho capito.** *(mee <u>skoo</u>-zee nohn oh kah-<u>pee</u>-toh)* (I'm sorry, I didn't understand.)
- ✔ **Può ripetere più lentamente, per favore?** *(poo-<u>oh</u> ree-<u>peh</u>-teh-reh pee-<u>oo</u> lehn-tah-<u>mehn</u>-teh pehr fah-<u>voh</u>-reh)* (Can you please repeat it more slowly?)

When someone does you a favor — explaining the way or giving you directions — you probably want to say thanks. That one's easy: **Mille grazie!** *(<u>meel</u>-leh <u>grah</u>-tsee-eh)* (Thanks a million!)

When giving and receiving directions, you need a command of **numeri ordinali** *(noo-meh-ree ohr-dee-nah-lee)* (ordinal numbers). See Chapter 3.

Asking how far something is

You may want to know how near or far you are from your destination. Here are some typical questions and responses:

> ✔ **Quant'è lontano?** *(koo-ahn-teh lohn-tah-noh)* (How far is it?)
>
> **Saranno cinque minuti.** *(sah-rahn-noh cheen-koo-eh mee-noo-tee)* (About five minutes.)
>
> ✔ **È molto lontano?** *(eh mohl-toh lohn-tah-noh)* (Is it very far?)
>
> **Circa un chilometro.** *(cheer-kah oon kee-loh-meh-troh)* (About one kilometer.)
>
> ✔ **No, un paio di minuti.** *(noh oon pah-yoh dee mee-noo-tee)* (No, a couple of minutes.)
>
> ✔ **Posso arrivarci a piedi?** *(pohs-soh ahr-ree-vahr-chee ah pee-eh-dee)* (Can I walk there?)
>
> **Certo, è molto vicino.** *(chehr-toh eh mohl-toh vee-chee-noh)* (Sure, it's very close.)
>
> **È un po' lontano.** *(eh oon poh lohn-tah-noh)* (It's a bit far away.)

Verbs on the move

You need to know certain verbs when trying to understand directions. These are some of the verbs you'll find handy for finding your way:

> ✔ **andare** *(ahn-dah-reh)* (to go)
>
> ✔ **girare a destra/a sinistra** *(jee-rah-reh ah deh-strah/ah see-nee-strah)* (to turn right/left)
>
> ✔ **prendere** *(prehn-deh-reh)* (to take)
>
> ✔ **proseguire** *(proh-seh-goo-ee-reh)* (to go on)

✔ **seguire** *(seh-goo-ee-reh)* (to follow)

✔ **tornare/indietro** *(tohr-nah-reh/een-dee-eh-troh)* (to go back)

Imperatives are useful verb forms to know in a variety of situations, including when you're trying to get around in unfamiliar territory. Table 9-2 lists the informal verb form followed by the formal verb form. Check out Chapter 2 for help on deciding whether to use the formal or informal form.

Table 9-2	Imperative Verbs	
Informal/ Formal	*Pronunciation*	*Translation*
Va/Vada!	vah/vah-dah	Go!
Gira/Giri!	jee-rah/jee-ree	Turn!
Prendi/ Prenda!	prehn-dee/prehn-dah	Take!
Prosegui/ Prosegua!	proh-seh-goo-ee/ proh-seh-goo-ah	Go on!
Segui/Segua!	seh-goo-ee/seh-goo-ah	Follow!
Torna/Torni!	tohr-nah/tohr-nee	Go back!
Attraversa/ Attraversi!	aht-trah-vehr-sah/ aht-trah-vehr-see	Cross!

Notice that the endings of these verbs vary, apparently without a consistent pattern. These aren't typing mistakes — they're determined by the ending of the infinitive form of the verb, *-are, -ere,* or *-ire* (see Chapter 2). You can simply believe us and memorize these verbs.

No doubt the most frequently used verb in giving and receiving instructions is **andare** *(ahn-dah-reh)* (to go), which we've conjugated for you in Table 9-3.

Table 9-3	Conjugating the Verb *Andare*	
Italian	*Pronunciation*	*Translation*
io vado	<u>ee</u>-oh <u>vah</u>-doh	I go
tu vai	too <u>vah</u>-ee	you (informal, singular) go
Lei va	lay vah	you (formal, singular) go
lui/lei va	<u>loo</u>-ee/lay vah	he/she goes
noi andiamo	<u>noh</u>-ee ahn-dee-<u>ah</u>-moh	we go
Voi/voi andate	<u>voh</u>-ee ahn-<u>dah</u>-teh	you (formal/informal, plural) go
loro vanno	<u>loh</u>-roh <u>vahn</u>-noh	they go

Locations you may be looking for

When you're searching for a specific place, these sentences can help you ask the right questions.

- ✔ **Mi sa dire dov'è la stazione?** *(mee sah <u>dee</u>-reh doh-<u>veh</u> lah stah-dzee-<u>oh</u>-neh)* (Can you tell me where the station is?)

- ✔ **Devo andare all'aeroporto.** *(<u>deh</u>-voh ahn-<u>dah</u>-reh ahl-lah-eh-roh-<u>pohr</u>-toh)* (I have to go to the airport.)

- ✔ **Sto cercando il teatro Argentina.** *(stoh chehr-<u>kahn</u>-doh eel teh-<u>ah</u>-troh ahr-jehn-<u>tee</u>-nah)* (I'm looking for the Argentina theater.)

- ✔ **Dov'è il cinema Astoria?** *(doh-<u>veh</u> eel <u>chee</u>-neh-mah ah-<u>stoh</u>-ree-ah)* (Where is the Astoria cinema?)

- ✔ **Come posso arrivare al Museo Romano?** *(<u>koh</u>-meh <u>pohs</u>-soh ahr-ree-<u>vah</u>-reh ahl moo-<u>zeh</u>-oh roh-<u>mah</u>-noh)* (How can I get to the Roman Museum?)

✔ **La strada migliore per il centro, per favore?** *(lah strah-dah mee-lyoh-reh pehr eel chehn-troh pehr fah-voh-reh)* (The best way to downtown, please?)

✔ **Che chiesa è questa?** *(keh kee-eh-zah eh koo-eh-stah)* (What church is this?)

✔ **Che autobus va all'ospedale?** *(keh ah-oo-toh-boos vah ahl-loh-speh-dah-leh)* (Which bus goes to the hospital?)

Words to Know

a destra	ah deh-strah	to the right
a sinistra	ah see-nee-strah	to the left
stazione [f]	stah-dzee-oh-neh	station
aeroporto [m]	ah-eh-roh-pohr-toh	airport
teatro [m]	teh-ah-troh	theater
cinema [m]	chee-neh-mah	cinema
duomo [m]	doo-oh-moh	cathedral
chiesa [f]	kee-eh-zah	church
ponte [m]	pohn-teh	bridge
piazza [f]	pee-aht-tsah	square
centro [m]	chehn-troh	downtown, city center
ospedale [m]	oh-speh-dah-leh	hospital
posta [f]	poh-stah	post office

Chapter 10

Finding a Place to Lay Your Weary Head

● ●

In This Chapter

▶ Booking a room

▶ Arriving at your hotel

▶ Using relative possessive pronouns

● ●

*I*f you're not lucky enough to have friends who can offer you a place to stay when you travel, you have to find a hotel. This chapter shows you how to make yourself understood when you ask for a room or check in. Plus, we give you a crash course on making plurals and using possessive pronouns.

Reserving a Room

When you reserve a room in a hotel, you use many of the same terms as you do when booking a table in a restaurant (see Chapter 5). Substitute either **la camera** *(lah kah-meh-rah)* or **la stanza** *(lah stahn-dzah),* both of which mean "the room," for **il tavolo** *(eel tah-voh-loh)* (the table).

The little differences between Italian and American hotel terms can cause big trouble if using the wrong ones means that you don't get what you want. So we want to tell you how to ask for what kind of room you want in Italian:

> ✔ **La camera singola** *(lah kah-meh-rah seen-goh-lah)* is a room with one bed.

> ✔ **La camera doppia** *(lah kah-meh-rah dohp-pee-ah)* is a room with two twin beds.

> ✔ **La camera matrimoniale** *(lah kah-meh-rah mah-tree-moh-nee-ah-leh)* has one big bed for two people.

In Italy, you choose not only your room type, but also what meals you want. You can opt for

> ✔ **La mezza pensione** *(lah meht-tsah pehn-see-oh-neh),* which includes breakfast and one hot meal (dinner in most cases).

> ✔ **La pensione completa** *(lah pehn-see-oh-neh kohm-pleh-tah),* which includes breakfast, lunch, and dinner.

We don't need to tell you that making reservations in advance is important — particularly for the **alta stagione** *(ahl-tah stah-joh-neh)* (high season). In Italy, high season is the summer months and the weeks around Easter. If you haven't reserved a room and have to request one when you arrive at the hotel, you may have to compromise.

When making reservations, you may have questions about the available rooms and the hotel's amenities. You'll probably encounter and use some of these common questions and phrases:

> ✔ **Avete stanze libere?** *(ah-veh-teh stahn-dzeh lee-beh-reh)* (Do you have any vacant rooms?)

> ✔ **La stanza è con bagno?** *(lah stahn-dzah eh kohn bah-nyoh)* (Does the room have a bathroom?)

> ✔ **Posso avere una stanza con doccia?** *(pohs-soh ah-veh-reh oo-nah stahn-dzah kohn dohch-chah)* (May I have a room with a shower?)

✔ **Non avete stanze con la vasca?** *(nohn ah-veh-teh stahn-tseh kohn lah vah-skah)* (Don't you have rooms with bathtubs?)

✔ **Avete una doppia al primo piano?** *(ah-veh-teh oo-nah dohp-pee-ah ahl pree-moh pee-ah-noh)* (Do you have a double room on the first floor?)

✔ **La colazione è compresa?** *(lah koh-lah-dzee-oh-neh eh kohm-preh-zah)* (Is breakfast included?)

✔ **Può darmi una camera con aria condizionata e televisione?** *(poo-oh dahr-mee oo-nah kah-meh-rah kohn ah-ree-ah kohn-dee-dzee-oh-nah-tah eh teh-leh-vee-zee-oh-neh)* (Can you give me a room with air conditioning and a television?)

✔ **C'è il telefono nella mia stanza?** *(cheh eel teh-leh-foh-noh nehl-lah mee-ah stahn-dzah)* (Is there a telephone in my room?)

The reservations agent might tell you something like this:

✔ **È una stanza tranquillissima e dà sul giardino.** *(eh oo-nah stahn-dzah trahn-koo-eel-lees-see-mah eh dah sool jahr-dee-noh)* (The room is very quiet and looks out onto the garden.)

✔ **La doppia viene centotrenta euro a notte.** *(lah dohp-pee-ah vee-eh-neh chehn-toh-trehn-tah eh-oo-roh ah noht-teh)* (A double room costs 130.00 euro per night.)

Words to Know

prenotazione [f]	preh-noh-tah-dzee-oh-neh	reservation
camera [f]	kah-meh-rah	room
stanza [f]	stahn-tsah	room
		continued

Words to Know *(continued)*

il soggiorno [m]	eel sohj-<u>johr</u>-noh	the stay
aria condizionata [f]	<u>ah</u>-ree-ah kohn-dee-dzee-oh-<u>nah</u>-tah	air conditioning
colazione [f]	koh-lah-dzee-<u>oh</u>-neh	breakfast
letto supplementare [m]	<u>leht</u>-toh soop-pleh-mehn-<u>tah</u>-reh	extra bed
per due notti	pehr <u>doo</u>-eh <u>noht</u>-tee	for two nights

Checking in and Getting Settled

One of the first things you do when checking into a hotel is attend to your luggage. The receptionist might ask **Dove sono i Suoi bagagli?** *(doh-veh soh-noh ee soo-oh-ee bah-gah-lyee)* (Where is your baggage?)

In response, you might ask **Può far portare le mie borse in camera, per favore?** *(poo-oh fahr pohr-tah-reh leh mee-eh bohr-seh een kah-meh-rah pehr fah-voh-reh)* (Can I have my bags brought to my room, please?)

Table 10-1 lists the conjugations for a couple of verbs that come in handy during a hotel stay — **portare** *(pohr-tah-reh)* (to bring) and **dare** *(dah-reh)* (to give).

Table 10-1	Conjugating the Verbs *Portare* and *Dare*	
Italian	*Pronunciation*	*Translation*
portare	**pohr-<u>tah</u>-reh**	**to bring**
io porto	<u>ee</u>-oh <u>pohr</u>-toh	I bring
tu porti	too <u>pohr</u>-tee	you (informal, singular) bring
Lei porta	lay <u>pohr</u>-tah	you (formal, singular) bring
lui/lei porta	<u>loo</u>-ee/lay <u>pohr</u>-tah	he/she brings
noi portiamo	<u>noh</u>-ee pohr-tee-<u>ah</u>-moh	we bring
Voi/voi portate	<u>voh</u>-ee pohr-<u>tah</u>-teh	you (formal/informal, plural) bring
loro portano	<u>loh</u>-roh <u>pohr</u>-tah-noh	they bring
dare	**<u>dah</u>-reh**	**to give**
io do	<u>ee</u>-oh doh	I give
tu dai	too <u>dah</u>-ee	you (informal, singular) give
Lei dà	lay dah	you (formal, singular) give
lui/lei dà	<u>loo</u>-ee/lay dah	he/she gives
noi diamo	<u>noh</u>-ee dee-<u>ah</u>-moh	we give
Voi/voi date	<u>voh</u>-ee <u>dah</u>-teh	you (formal/informal, plural) give
loro danno	<u>loh</u>-roh <u>dahn</u>-noh	they give

After you begin unpacking, you may find that you forgot to bring something you need. Or you may want some special amenity, like **una cassaforte** *(oo-nah kahs-sah-fohr-teh)* (a safe) for your valuables or **un frigorifero** *(oon free-goh-ree-feh-roh)* (a refrigerator). In these instances, you're likely to ask the front desk or the maid for what you need. The following phrases can help you:

- ✔ **Non trovo l'asciugacapelli.** *(nohn troh-voh lah-shoo-gah-kah-pehl-lee)* (I can't find the hair dryer.)

- ✔ **Gli asciugamani devono essere cambiati e manca la carta igenica.** *(lyee ah-shoo-gah-mah-nee deh-voh-noh ehs-seh-reh kahm-bee-ah-tee eh mahn-kah lah kahr-tah ee-jeh-nee-kah)* (The towels must be changed and there is no toilet paper.)

- ✔ **Potrei avere un'altra saponetta?** *(poh-tray ah-veh-reh oon-ahl-trah sah-poh-neht-tah)* (May I have a new soap?)

  If you want something else, notice that you write the feminine form **un'altra** *(oon-ahl-trah)* differently than the masculine **un altro** *(oon ahl-troh)*. Feminine words that begin with a vowel require an apostrophe after the article; masculine words that begin with a vowel don't.

- ✔ **Ho finito lo shampo.** *(oh fee-nee-toh loh shahm-poh)* (I ran out of shampoo.)

- ✔ **Vorrei un'altra coperta e due cuscini, per favore.** *(vohr-ray oon-ahl-trah koh-pehr-tah eh doo-eh koo-shee-nee pehr fah-voh-reh)* (I'd like one more blanket and two pillows, please.)

- ✔ **Vorrei la sveglia domattina.** *(vohr-ray lah sveh-lyah doh-maht-tee-nah)* (I'd like to get an early wake-up call tomorrow morning.)

Table 10-2 contains some additional words that you may find useful during a hotel stay.

Table 10-2	Useful Hotel Vocabulary	
Italian	*Pronunciation*	*Translation*
asciugacapelli [m]	ah-shoo-gah-kah-<u>pehl</u>-lee	hair dryer
chiave [f]	kee-<u>ah</u>-veh	key
fazzolettino di carta [m]	faht-tsoh-leht-<u>tee</u>-noh dee <u>kahr</u>-tah	tissue
lettino [m]	leht-<u>tee</u>-noh	cot
negozio di regali [m]	neh-<u>goh</u>-dzee-oh dee reh-<u>gah</u>-lee	gift shop
portacenere [m]	pohr-tah-<u>cheh</u>-neh-reh	ashtray
piscina [f]	pee-<u>shee</u>-nah	swimming pool
servizio in camera [m]	sehr-<u>vee</u>-dzee-oh een <u>kah</u>-meh-rah	room service
servizio sveglia [m]	sehr-<u>vee</u>-dzee-oh <u>sveh</u>-lyah	wake-up call

Words to Know

avete	ah-<u>veh</u>-teh	do you (plural) have
dov'è	doh-<u>veh</u>	where is
dove sono	<u>doh</u>-veh <u>soh</u>-noh	where are
Può ripetere per favore?	poo-<u>oh</u> ree-<u>peh</u>-teh-reh pehr fah-<u>voh</u>-reh	Could you repeat that please?
saldare il conto	sahl-<u>dah</u>-reh eel <u>kohn</u>-toh	to check out

Using Plurals and Pronouns

Digging a little bit deeper into grammar can help you understand Italian better. In this section, we hope to improve your knowledge of Italian plurals and pronouns.

Making more in Italian

You may have noticed that the plural form in Italian isn't as simple as it is in English. In English, you usually add an *s* to the end of a word to make it plural. In Italian, how you make a noun plural depends on both the gender of the word and, as far as the article is concerned, on the first letters in the word. (Check out Chapter 2 for more on the gender of nouns.)

Italian nouns are either masculine or feminine. You use a different article with each gender:

✔ The masculine articles **il** *(eel)* and **lo** *(loh)* accompany masculine nouns, most of which end in *o.*

✔ The feminine article **la** *(lah)* accompanies feminine nouns, most of which end in *a.*

Masculine nouns that begin with a vowel, such as **l'amico** (*lah-mee-koh*) (the friend), or any of the following consonants take the article **lo** *(loh):*

✔ *z,* as in **lo zio** *(loh dzee-oh)* (uncle)

✔ *gn,* as in **lo gnomo** *(loh nyoh-moh)* (the gnome)

✔ *y,* as in **lo yogurt** *(loh yoh-goort)* (the yogurt)

✔ *s* followed by another consonant (*sb, sc, sd,* and so on), as in **lo studente** *(loh stoo-dehn-teh)* (the student)

When the word begins with a vowel, **lo** is abbreviated as **l'**, as in **l'amico.** The same is true for feminine nouns that begin with a vowel; **la** is reduced to **l'**. There is no

feminine equivalent to the masculine **lo.** In the plural,
lo and **l'** (for masculine nouns) become **gli** *(lyee).*

When you understand these rules, forming plurals is
easy:

✔ For a feminine noun, such as **la cameriera** *(lah
kah-meh-ree-eh-rah)* (the chambermaid) or **l'entrata** *(lehn-trah-tah)* (the hall), change the final *a*
(in the article as well as the word) to *e* so that **la
cameriera** becomes **le cameriere** *(leh kah-meh-
ree-eh-reh)* and **l'entrata** becomes **le entrate**
(leh ehn-trah-teh).

✔ For a masculine noun, such as **il bagno** *(eel bah-
nyoh)* (bathroom), the plural article becomes **i**
(ee), and so does the final **o** of the word. So **il
bagno** becomes **i bagni** *(ee bah-nyee).*

✔ With some exceptions, to make nouns ending in *e*
plural — for example, **la chiave** *(lah kee-ah-veh)*
(the key) and **il cameriere** *(eel kah-meh-ree-eh-
reh)* (the waiter) — you change the *e* to *i,* and the
article changes according to the gender — for
example, **le chiavi** *(leh kee-ah-vee)* (the keys)
and **i camerieri** *(ee kah-meh-ree-eh-ree)* (the wait-
ers). The masculine articles **lo** and **l'** change to
gli *(lyee),* and the feminine **l'** becomes **le** *(leh).*

Table 10-3 shows the plural forms of several hotel-
related words.

Table 10-3	Making Plurals	
Italian	*Pronunciation*	*Translation*
la cameriera [f]	lah kah-meh-ree-eh-rah	chambermaid
le cameriere [f]	leh kah-meh-ree-eh-reh	chambermaids
il bagno [m]	eel bah-nyoh	bathroom
i bagni [m]	ee bah-nyee	bathrooms

(continued)

Table 10-3 *(continued)*

Italian	Pronunciation	Translation
la chiave [f]	lah kee-<u>ah</u>-veh	key
le chiavi [f]	leh kee-<u>ah</u>-vee	keys
il cameriere [m]	eel kah-meh-ree-<u>eh</u>-reh	waiter
i camerieri [m]	ee kah-meh-ree-<u>eh</u>-ree	waiters
lo specchio [m]	loh <u>spehk</u>-kee-oh	mirror
gli specchi [m]	lyee <u>spehk</u>-kee	mirrors
l'albergo [m]	lahl-<u>behr</u>-goh	hotel
gli alberghi [m]	lyee ahl-<u>behr</u>-gee	hotels
la stanza [f]	lah <u>stahn</u>-dzah	room
le stanze [f]	leh <u>stahn</u>-dzeh	rooms
la camera [f]	lah <u>kah</u>-meh-rah	room
le camere [f]	leh <u>kah</u>-meh-reh	rooms
la persona [f]	lah pehr-<u>soh</u>-nah	person
le persone [f]	leh pehr-<u>soh</u>-neh	persons/people
il letto [m]	eel <u>leht</u>-toh	bed
i letti [m]	ee <u>leht</u>-tee	beds
la notte [f]	lah <u>noht</u>-teh	night
le notti [f]	leh <u>noht</u>-tee	nights
l'entrata [f]	lehn-<u>trah</u>-tah	hall
le entrate [f]	leh ehn-<u>trah</u>-teh	halls

Personalizing pronouns

As you know, a pronoun is a word that you use in place of a noun, such as *I.* Sometimes you use a pronoun that not only takes the place of a noun but also indicates to whom it belongs. For example, when you say "My bag is red and yours is black," the possessive pronoun *yours* represents the word *bag* and indicates to whom the bag belongs.

In English, you use the pronouns *this* and *these* (called demonstrative pronouns) to indicate what you're talking about. You can use *this* or *these* with any noun as long as you get the number right: this book, these girls, and so on. In Italian, however, which word you use depends on both number and gender because there are masculine and feminine articles. Consider these examples:

✔ **Questa è la Sua valigia?** *(koo-eh-stah eh lah soo-ah vah-lee-jah)* (Is this your suitcase?)

✔ **No, le mie sono queste.** *(noh leh mee-eh soh-noh koo-eh-steh)* (No, these are mine.)

Here you see the feminine version of singular and plural (**questa** and **queste,** respectively). The following shows the masculine version of singular and plural (**questo** and **questi**):

✔ **Signore, questo messaggio è per Lei.** *(see-nyoh-reh koo-eh-stoh mehs-sahj-joh eh pehr lay)* (Sir, this message is for you.)

✔ **Questi prezzi sono eccessivi!** *(koo-eh-stee preht-tsee soh-noh ehch-chehs-see-vee)* (These prices are excessive!)

Possessive pronouns such as *my, your,* and *his* indicate possession of something (the noun). In Italian, the possessive pronoun varies according to the gender of the item it refers to. The possessive pronoun must agree in number and gender with the possessed thing or person. Unlike in English, in Italian you almost always put the article in front of the possessive determiner.

When you want to show that something belongs to you and that something is a feminine noun, the possessive **mia** ends in *a,* such as **la mia valigia** *(lah mee-ah vah-lee-jah)* (my suitcase). When you refer to a masculine word, the possessive ends in *o,* as in **il mio letto** *(eel mee-oh leht-toh)* (my bed).

So these pronouns get their form from the possessor — **il mio** *(eel mee-oh)* (mine), **il tuo** *(eel too-oh)* (yours, informal), and so on — and their number and gender from the thing possessed. For example, in **è la mia chiave** *(eh lah mee-ah kee-ah-veh)* (it's my key), **la chiave** is singular and feminine and therefore is replaced by the possessive pronoun **mia.** Table 10-4 lists the possessive pronouns and their articles.

Table 10-4	Possessive Pronouns			
Possessive Pronoun	Singular Masculine Object	Singular Feminine Object	Plural Masculine Objects	Plural Feminine Objects
my/mine	il mio	la mia	i miei	le mie
your/yours (informal, singular person)	il tuo	la tua	i tuoi	le tue
your/yours (formal, singular person)	il Suo	la Sua	i Suoi	le Sue
his/her/ hers	il suo	la sua	i suoi	le sue
our/ours	il nostro	la nostra	i nostri	le nostre

Possessive Pronoun	Singular Masculine Object	Singular Feminine Object	Plural Masculine Objects	Plural Feminine Objects
your/yours (formal/informal, plural persons)	il Vostro/ vostro	la Vostra/ vostra	i Vostri/ vostri	le Vostre/ vostre
their/theirs	il loro	la loro	i loro	le loro

Following are some practical examples using possessive pronouns:

✔ **È grande la vostra stanza?** *(eh <u>grahn</u>-deh lah <u>voh</u>-strah <u>stahn</u>-dzah)* (Is your [informal, plural persons] room large?)

✔ **Dov'è il tuo albergo?** *(doh-<u>veh</u> eel <u>too</u>-oh ahl-<u>behr</u>-goh)* (Where is your [informal, singular person] hotel?)

✔ **Ecco i Vostri documenti.** *(<u>ehk</u>-koh ee <u>voh</u>-stree doh-koo-<u>mehn</u>-tee)* (Here are your [formal, plural persons] documents.)

✔ **Questa è la Sua chiave.** *(koo-<u>eh</u>-stah eh lah <u>soo</u>-ah kee-<u>ah</u>-veh)* (This is your [formal, singular person] key.)

✔ **Questa è la sua chiave.** *(koo-<u>eh</u>-stah eh lah <u>soo</u>-ah kee-<u>ah</u>-veh)* (This is his/her key.)

✔ **La mia camera è molto tranquilla.** *(lah <u>mee</u>-ah <u>kah</u>-meh-rah eh <u>mohl</u>-toh trahn-koo-<u>eel</u>-lah)* (My room is very quiet.)

✔ **Anche la nostra. E la tua?** *(<u>ahn</u>-keh lah <u>noh</u>-strah eh lah <u>too</u>-ah)* (Ours too. And yours [informal, singular person]?)

Words to Know

bagaglio [m]	bah-_gah_-lyoh	baggage
borsa [f]	_bohr_-sah	bag
cameriera [f]	kah-meh-ree-_eh_-rah	chambermaid
garage [m]	gah-_rahj_	car park, garage
messaggio [m]	mehs-_sahj_-joh	message
portiere [m]	pohr-tee-_eh_-reh	doorman
valigia [f]	vah-_lee_-jah	suitcase

Chapter 11

Dealing with Emergencies

● ●

In This Chapter

▶ Asking for help

▶ Dealing with car troubles

▶ Describing what ails you

▶ Protecting your legal rights

● ●

*A*sking for help is never fun, but if you're in a jam, you need to know how to communicate what you need. In case you find yourself facing car trouble, illness, or legal trouble, we give you the words and phrases you need to communicate your woes to the people who can help.

Table 11-1 gives a general sampling of things you can say when you need help.

Table 11-1	Asking for Help	
Italian	*Pronunciation*	*Translation*
Aiuto!	ah-<u>yoo</u>-toh	Help!
Mi aiuti, per favore.	mee ah-<u>yoo</u>-tee pehr fah-<u>voh</u>-reh	Help me, please.
Chiamate la polizia!	kee-ah-<u>mah</u>-teh lah poh-lee-<u>dzee</u>-ah	Call the police!

(continued)

Table 11-1 *(continued)*

Italian	Pronunciation	Translation
Ho bisogno di un medico.	oh bee-<u>zoh</u>-nyoh dee oon <u>meh</u>-dee-koh	I need a doctor.
Chiamate un'ambulanza!	kee-ah-<u>mah</u>-teh oo-nahm-boo-<u>lahn</u>-dzah	Call an ambulance!

As you may have noticed, you conjugate sentences directed at a group of people in the plural form (see Chapter 2 for more on conjugating verbs in Italian). In an emergency situation, you address your cries for help to anyone who may be listening.

In some situations, you must ask for a competent authority who speaks English. Do so by using one of the following phrases:

- ✔ **Mi scusi, parla inglese?** *(mee <u>skoo</u>-zee <u>pahr</u>-lah een-<u>gleh</u>-zeh)* (Excuse me, do you speak English?)

- ✔ **C'è un medico che parli inglese?** *(cheh oon <u>meh</u>-dee-koh keh <u>pahr</u>-lee een-<u>gleh</u>-zeh)* (Is there a doctor who speaks English?)

- ✔ **Dove posso trovare un avvocato che parli inglese?** *(<u>doh</u>-veh <u>pohs</u>-soh troh-<u>vah</u>-reh oon ahv-voh-<u>kah</u>-toh keh <u>pahr</u>-lee een-<u>gleh</u>-zeh)* (Where can I find a lawyer who speaks English?)

If you can't find a professional who speaks English, you may be able to find **un interprete** *(oon een-<u>tehr</u>-preh-teh)* (an interpreter) to help you.

Dealing with Car Trouble

If you have car trouble, you need to call a mechanic who can help you out of the situation. Table 11-2 lists some vocabulary that you can use to explain your problem.

Table 11-2	Calling a Mechanic	
Italian	*Pronunciation*	*Translation*
aiuto [m]	ah-<u>yoo</u>-toh	help
fermare	fehr-<u>mah</u>-reh	to stop
Mi si è fermata la macchina.	mee see eh fehr-<u>mah</u>-tah lah <u>mahk</u>-kee-nah	My car broke down.
il più presto possible	eel pee-<u>oo</u> <u>preh</u>-stoh pohs-<u>see</u>-bee-leh	as soon as possible
soccorso stradale [m]	sohk-<u>kohr</u>-soh strah-<u>dah</u>-leh	roadside assistance
traffico [m]	<u>trahf</u>-fee-koh	traffic
meccanico [m]	mehk-<u>kah</u>-nee-koh	mechanic
carro attrezzi [m]	<u>kahr</u>-roh aht-<u>treht</u>-tsee	tow truck

If a traffic accident occurs, you need to find help right away. Table 11-3 lists some words to use in this situation.

Table 11-3	Summoning Help after an Accident	
Italian	*Pronunciation*	*Translation*
C'è un incidente.	cheh oon een-chee-<u>dehn</u>-teh	There's been an accident.
C'è un ferito.	cheh oon fehr-<u>ee</u>-toh	Someone is injured.
ambulanza [f]	ahm-boo-<u>lahn</u>-dzah	ambulance
emergenza [f]	eh-mehr-<u>jehn</u>-dzah	emergency
Fate presto, è urgente!	<u>fah</u>-teh <u>preh</u>-stoh eh oor-<u>jehn</u>-teh	Hurry, it's urgent!

Words to Know

macchina [f]	<u>mahk</u>-kee-nah	car
incidente stradale [m]	een-chee-<u>dehn</u>-teh strah-<u>dah</u>-leh	traffic accident
denunciare	deh-noon-<u>chah</u>-reh	to report
danno [m]	<u>dahn</u>-noh	damage
ferita [f]	feh-<u>ree</u>-tah	injury
assicurazione [f]	ahs-see-koo-rah-dzee-<u>oh</u>-neh	insurance

Talking to Doctors

If you need to tell someone that you're not feeling well, you can always say **mi sento male** *(mee <u>sehn</u>-toh <u>mah</u>-leh)* (I feel sick), which derives from the verb and adjective combination **sentirsi male** *(sehn-<u>teer</u>-see <u>mah</u>-leh)* (to feel sick). Table 11-4 gives you the whole conjugation.

Table 11-4   Conjugating the Verb *Sentirsi [Male]*

Italian	Pronunciation	Translation
mi sento [male]	mee <u>sehn</u>-toh <u>mah</u>-leh	I feel [sick]
ti senti [male]	tee <u>sehn</u>-tee <u>mah</u>-leh	you (informal, singular) feel [sick]
Si sente [male]	see <u>sehn</u>-teh <u>mah</u>-leh	you (formal, singular) feel [sick]
si sente [male]	see <u>sehn</u>-teh <u>mah</u>-leh	he/she feels [sick]

Italian	Pronunciation	Translation
ci sentiamo [male]	chee sehn-tee-_ah_-moh _mah_-leh	we feel [sick]
Vi/vi sentite [male]	vee sehn-_tee_-teh _mah_-leh	you (formal/informal, plural) feel [sick]
si sentono [male]	see _sehn_-toh-noh _mah_-leh	they feel [sick]

When you're in **l'ospedale** *(loh-speh-_dah_-leh)* (the hospital) or at **il medico** *(eel _meh_-dee-koh)* (the doctor), you need to be more precise. You can choose one of two expressions to describe what ails you:

✔ **fare male** *(_fah_-reh _mah_-leh)* (to hurt)

✔ **avere mal di** *(ah-_veh_-reh mahl dee)* (to hurt)

The latter is the easier way to express your ailments, because you only have to know the **ho** *(oh)* (I have) form of the verb **avere** *(ah-_veh_-reh)* (to have). You simply add the name of the body part that hurts, like this:

Ho mal di testa. *(oh mahl dee _teh_-stah)* (I have a headache.)

Fare male is a little bit trickier because the subject is the aching part or parts. If your head hurts, you can say

Mi fa male la testa. *(mee fah _mah_-leh lah _teh_-stah)* (My head hurts.)

If more than one part aches, you must use the plural verb form:

Mi fanno male il collo e le spalle. *(mee _fahn_-noh _mah_-leh eel _kohl_-loh eh leh _spahl_-leh)* (My neck and shoulders hurt.)

You may have noticed that **fa male** is preceded by **mi** *(mee)* (me). This word changes according to the speaker — the person who feels the pain. A doctor may ask you **Cosa Le fa male?** *(koh-zah leh fah mah-leh)* (What hurts you?). **Le** is the indirect object pronoun for the formal "you." (See Chapter 2 for more on indirect object pronouns.)

Table 11-5 gives you the Italian words for various body parts.

Table 11-5	Basic Body Parts	
Italian	*Pronunciation*	*Translation*
il braccio [m]	eel <u>brahch</u>-choh	the arm
il collo [m]	eel <u>kohl</u>-loh	the neck
il corpo [m]	eel <u>kohr</u>-poh	the body
il dito [m]	eel <u>dee</u>-toh	the finger
la gamba [f]	lah <u>gahm</u>-bah	the leg
il ginocchio [m]	eel jee-<u>nohk</u>-kee-oh	the knee
la mano [f]	lah <u>mah</u>-noh	the hand
l'orecchio [m]	loh-<u>rehk</u>-kee-oh	the ear
la pancia [f]	lah <u>pahn</u>-chah	the belly
il petto [m]	eel <u>peht</u>-toh	the breast
il piede [m]	eel pee-<u>eh</u>-deh	the foot
la spalla [f]	lah <u>spahl</u>-lah	the shoulder
lo stomaco [m]	loh <u>stoh</u>-mah-koh	the stomach
la testa [f]	lah <u>teh</u>-stah	the head

The following phrases can help you put those body parts and a few others in context for the doctor or nurse:

- ✔ **Mi sono rotto una gamba.** *(mee soh-noh roht-toh oo-nah gahm-bah)* (I broke a leg.)

- ✔ **Ho la gola arrossata.** *(oh lah goh-lah ahr-rohs-sah-tah)* (I have a sore throat.)

- ✔ **Ho la pelle irritata.** *(oh lah pehl-leh eer-ree-tah-tah)* (My skin is irritated.)

- ✔ **Mi sono storto il piede.** *(mee soh-noh stohr-toh eel pee-eh-deh)* (I sprained my foot.)

- ✔ **Ho mal di schiena.** *(oh mahl dee skee-eh-nah)* (I have a backache.)

- ✔ **Ho disturbi al cuore.** *(oh dee-stoor-bee ahl koo-oh-reh)* (I have heart problems.)

- ✔ **Il dentista mi ha tolto un dente.** *(eel dehn-tee-stah mee ah tohl-toh oon dehn-teh)* (The dentist pulled out my tooth.)

- ✔ **Mi fa male lo stomaco.** *(mee fah mah-leh loh stoh-mah-koh)* (My stomach hurts.)

- ✔ **Mi bruciano gli occhi.** *(mee broo-chah-noh lyee ohk-kee)* (My eyes burn.)

- ✔ **Mi sono slogata la spalla.** *(mee soh-noh sloh-gah-tah lah spahl-lah)* (I've dislocated my shoulder.)

- ✔ **Ho mal di testa.** *(oh mahl dee teh-stah)* (I have a headache.)

- ✔ **Mi fa male tutto il corpo.** *(mee fah mah-leh toot-toh eel kohr-poh)* (My whole body aches.)

When you want to indicate the left or right body part, you must know that body part's gender:

- ✔ For a masculine part, you say **destro** *(deh-stroh)* (right) or **sinistro** *(see-nee-stroh)* (left).

- ✔ For a feminine part, you change the ending: **destra** *(deh-strah)* or **sinistra** *(see-nee-strah)*.

Where body parts are concerned, Italian has lots of irregular plurals. Table 11-6 lists some of the most common irregular plural forms.

Table 11-6	Irregular Plural Body Parts	
Italian	*Pronunciation*	*Translation*
le braccia	leh <u>brahch</u>-chah	arms
le dita	leh <u>dee</u>-tah	fingers
le ginocchia	leh jee-<u>nohk</u>-kee-ah	knees
le mani	leh <u>mah</u>-nee	hands
le orecchie	leh oh-<u>rehk</u>-kee-eh	ears
le ossa	leh <u>ohs</u>-sah	bones

Words to Know

ospedale [m]	oh-speh-<u>dah</u>-leh	hospital
medico [m]	<u>meh</u>-dee-koh	doctor
dentista [m]	dehn-<u>tee</u>-stah	dentist
raggi [m]	<u>rahj</u>-jee	X-rays
sinistra/o [f/m]	see-<u>nee</u>-strah/-stroh	left
destra/o [f/m]	<u>deh</u>-strah/-stroh	right
gonfia/o [f/m]	<u>gohn</u>-fee-ah/-oh	swollen
ricetta [f]	ree-<u>cheht</u>-tah	prescription
medicina [f]	meh-dee-<u>chee</u>-nah	medicine
farmacia [f]	fahr-mah-<u>chee</u>-ah	pharmacy

I've Been Robbed! Knowing What to Do and Say When the Police Arrive

We hope that you're never the victim of a robbery. If you are, however, you need to be prepared with certain important phrases when the police arrive. Here are some key phrases:

- ✔ **Sono stata/o derubata/o.** *(soh-noh stah-tah/-toh deh-roo-bah-tah/-toh)* (I've been robbed. [f/m])

- ✔ **C'è stato un furto nel mio appartamento.** *(cheh stah-toh oon foor-toh nehl mee-oh ahp-pahr-tah-mehn-toh)* (There was a burglary in my apartment.)

- ✔ **Sono entrati dei ladri in casa nostra.** *(soh-noh ehn-trah-tee day lah-dree een kah-sah noh-strah)* (Thieves broke into our house.)

- ✔ **Mi hanno rubato la macchina.** *(mee ahn-noh roo-bah-toh lah mahk-kee-nah)* (My car has been stolen.)

- ✔ **Mi hanno scippata.** *(mee ahn-noh sheep-pah-tah)* (My handbag was snatched.)

- ✔ **Dov'è la questura?** *(doh-veh lah koo-eh-stoo-rah)* (Where is the police headquarters?)

When you have to report a theft, you need to know how to describe some essential physical characteristics, such as hair color and height. You form descriptive sentences like this:

La persona era . . . *(lah pehr-soh-nah eh-rah)* (The person was . . .):

- ✔ **alta** *(ahl-tah)* (tall)

- ✔ **bassa** *(bahs-sah)* (short)

- ✔ **di media statura** *(dee meh-dee-ah stah-too-rah)* (of medium build)

- **grassa** *(grahs-sah)* (fat)
- **magra** *(mah-grah)* (thin)

Note: The preceding adjectives end in *-a* because they refer to the noun **la persona,** which is feminine.

I capelli erano . . . *(ee kah-pehl-lee eh-rah-noh)* (The hair was . . .)

- **castani** *(kah-stah-nee)* (brown)
- **biondi** *(byohn-dee)* (blond)
- **neri** *(neh-ree)* (black)
- **rossi** *(rohs-see)* (red)
- **scuri** *(skoo-ree)* (dark)
- **chiari** *(kee-ah-ree)* (light)
- **lisci** *(lee-shee)* (straight)
- **ondulati** *(ohn-doo-lah-tee)* (wavy)
- **ricci** *(reech-chee)* (curly)
- **corti** *(kohr-tee)* (short)
- **lunghi** *(loon-gee)* (long)

Aveva gli occhi . . . *(ah-veh-vah lyee ohk-kee)* (The eyes were . . .)

- **azzurri** *(aht-tsoor-ree)* (blue)
- **grigi** *(gree-jee)* (gray)
- **marroni** *(mahr-roh-nee)* (brown)
- **verdi** *(vehr-dee)* (green)
- **neri** *(neh-ree)* (dark)

Era . . . *(eh-rah)* (He was . . .)

- **calvo** *(kahl-voh)* (bald)
- **rasato** *(rah-zah-toh)* (clean shaven)

Aveva . . . *(ah-veh-vah)* (He had . . .)

| ✔ **la barba** *(lah bahr-bah)* (a beard)
| ✔ **i baffi** *(ee bahf-fee)* (a moustache)

When You Need a Lawyer

Many unpleasant moments in life require that you seek the help of an authorized person, such as a lawyer. Therefore, knowing how to contact a lawyer is rather important. You can use these general questions and statements:

✔ **Mi serve l'aiuto di un avvocato.** *(mee sehr-veh lah-yoo-toh dee oon ahv-voh-kah-toh)* (I need the help of a lawyer.)

✔ **Ho bisogno di assistenza legale.** *(oh bee-zoh-nyoh dee ahs-see-stehn-dzah leh-gah-leh)* (I need legal assistance.)

✔ **Vorrei consultare il mio avvocato.** *(vohr-ray kohn-sool-tah-reh eel mee-oh ahv-voh-kah-toh)* (I'd like to consult my lawyer.)

✔ **Chiamate il mio avvocato, per favore.** *(kee-ah-mah-teh eel mee-oh ahv-voh-kah-toh pehr fah-voh-reh)* (Call my lawyer, please.)

After you find a lawyer, you can speak to him or her about your situation. Table 11-7 lists some examples of what you may need to say.

Table 11-7	Explaining Your Legal Troubles	
Italian	*Pronunciation*	*Translation*
Sono stato truffato.	soh-noh stah-toh troof-fah-toh	I was cheated.
Voglio denunciare un furto.	Voh-lyoh deh-noon-chah-reh oon foor-toh	I want to report a theft.

(continued)

Table 11-7 *(continued)*

Italian	Pronunciation	Translation
Devo stipulare un contratto.	<u>deh</u>-voh stee-poo-<u>lah</u>-reh oon kohn-<u>traht</u>-toh	I have to negotiate a contract.
Ho avuto un incidente stradale.	oh ah-<u>voo</u>-toh oon een-chee-<u>dehn</u>-teh strah-<u>dah</u>-leh	I've had a traffic accident.
Voglio che mi vengano risarciti i danni.	<u>voh</u>-lyoh keh mee <u>vehn</u>-gah-noh ree-sahr-<u>chee</u>-tee ee <u>dahn</u>-nee	I want to be compensated for the damages.
Sono stato arrestato.	<u>soh</u>-noh <u>stah</u>-toh ahr-reh-<u>stah</u>-toh	I've been arrested.

Chapter 12

Ten Favorite Italian Expressions

● ●

Mamma mia! (My goodness!)

Don't think that Italians are like children because they call for their mommies so often. Italians use **Mamma mia!** (*mahm-mah mee-ah*) to express surprise, impatience, happiness, sorrow — any strong emotion.

Che bello! (How lovely!)

Using this phrase, pronounced *keh behl-loh*, shows that you're enthusiastic about something.

Uffa! (Aargh!)

Uffa! (*oof-fah*) is a clear way to show that you're annoyed, bored, angry, or fed up.

Che ne so! (How should I know?)

When Italians want to say that they have no idea, they shrug their shoulders and say **Che ne so!** (*keh neh soh*).

Magari! (If only!)

Magari (*mah-gah-ree*) is just one word, but it expresses a lot. It indicates a strong wish or hope. It's a good answer if, for instance, somebody asks you if you'd like to win the lottery.

Ti sta bene! (Serves you right!)

Ti sta bene! *(tee stah beh-neh)* is the Italian way to say "Serves you right!"

Non te la prendere! (Don't get so upset! / Don't think about it!)

If you see that somebody is sad, worried, or upset, you can try to console him by saying **Non te la prendere!** *(nohn teh lah prehn-deh-reh)*.

Che macello! (What a mess!)

Figuring out the derivation of **Che macello!** *(keh mah-chehl-loh)* isn't difficult. The literal translation is "What a slaughterhouse!"

Non mi va! (I don't feel like it!)

Non mi va! *(nohn mee vah)* is one of the first phrases that Italian children learn. It means that you don't want to do something.

Mi raccomando! (Please, I beg you!)

With **Mi raccomando!** *(mee rahk-koh-mahn-doh)*, you express a special emphasis in asking for something. An example is **Telefonami, mi raccomando!** (Don't forget to call me, please!)

Chapter 13

Ten Phrases That Make You Sound Like a Local

• •

In bocca al lupo! (Good luck!)

Perhaps you have a friend facing a difficult task and you want to wish him good luck. **Buona fortuna** *(boo-oh-nah fohr-too-nah)* would work, but **In bocca al lupo** *(een bohk-kah ahl loo-poh)* really makes you sound Italian. Literally, it means "in the wolf's mouth!" The upcoming difficulty looks like a big wolf, waiting with mouth open wide. Your friend will probably answer **Crepi il lupo** *(kreh-pee eel loo-poh),* which means "Hopefully the wolf will die!"

Acqua in bocca! (Don't say a word!)

When you want to share a secret with someone but want to make sure that she won't tell anyone else, say **Acqua in bocca!** *(ahk-koo-ah een bohk-kah),* which means "water in mouth." (Implying, if your mouth is full of water, you can't speak.)

Salute! (Bless you!)

When someone sneezes, you say **Salute!** *(sah-loo-teh),* which means "health." Saying this word is a way to wish the person good health.

Macché! (Of course not! / Certainly not!)

Italians love to talk, but in some situations, they prefer to say just one word: **macché!** *(mahk-keh)*. It's a strong and determined way to say "Of course not!" or "Certainly not!"

Neanche per sogno! (In your dreams!)

Neanche per sogno *(neh-ahn-keh pehr soh-nyoh)* literally means "not even in a dream." It's a way to say "No way!"

Peggio per te! (Too bad for you!)

You don't show much sympathy when uttering this phrase, but if you're looking for the Italian equivalent of "too bad for you," then **peggio per te** *(pehj-joh pehr teh)* is what you need.

Piantala! (Stop it!)

The literal translation of **piantala** *(pee-ahn-tah-lah)*, an informal expression, is "Plant it!"

Vacci piano! (Slow down! / Take it easy!)

Use **vacci piano!** *(vahch-chee pee-ah-noh)* when you feel that somebody is going too fast or being overly enthusiastic about something.

Gatta ci cova! (There's something fishy going on!)

La gatta is the female cat, and **covare** means "to brood." When Italians say **gatta ci cova** (*gaht-tah chee koh-vah*) (a female cat is brooding here), they mean "There's something fishy going on here."

Sono nel pallone! (I'm flustered!)

People say **sono nel pallone** (*soh-noh nehl pahl-loh-neh*) to indicate that someone doesn't know what to do or how to behave in a difficult situation. **Sono** is "I am," and **pallone** means "ball," but also "balloon": Perhaps it means that the person feels up in the air?

Index

• **A** •

"a" vowel pronunciation, 10
accents, 16–17
accessories shopping, 108
accidents, help in, 179
acquainted, getting, 73–84
addresses. *See also* numbers
    e-mail, 55
    home description, 56
    street, 56
    verbs for, 57–58
    words related to, 55
adjectives. *See also* nouns;
        pronouns; verbs
    changes according to
        nouns, 24
    meaning change examples,
        24–25
    noun number/gender and, 23
    position, 24
airports. *See also* transportation
    check-in, 146–147
    customs, 148–149
    post-landing, 148
    pre-boarding, 147
animals, 126
annoyance phrase, 189
articles
    feminine, definite, 21–22
    feminine, indefinite, 23
    masculine, definite, 22
    masculine, indefinite, 23
assumptions, this book, 3

• **B** •

"b" consonant pronunciation, 11
baked goods, 113
banks. *See also* money
    employee conversations, 59
    investments, 60
    reasons for traveling to, 59
    words to know, 60

beg pardon, 69, 158
body parts. *See also* doctors;
        medical emergencies
    basic, 182
    feminine, 183
    irregular plural, 184
    masculine, 183
    in phrases, 183
breakfast. *See also* dining; meals
    barista and, 92
    habits, 92
    words to know, 92–93
buses. *See also* transportation
    big, 153
    little, 153
    schedules, 154
    ticket purchases, 153
    words to know, 154

• **C** •

"c" consonant pronunciation,
        12–13
car rentals. *See also*
        transportation
    conversation, 149–150
    process, 149
    terms/phrases, 150–151
car trouble
    help after accident, 179
    mechanics, calling, 179
    words to know, 180
cardinal numbers. *See also*
        numbers
    defined, 45
    irregular, 48
    list of, 46–48
cellphones, 138
changing money, 61
check-in, hotel. *See also* hotels
    phrases, 168
    questions/answers, 166
    verbs for, 166–167
    words to know, 169

clothing. *See also* shopping
  accessories, 108
  colors, 106–107
  fabrics, 107–108
  shoes, 109
  shopping, 104–109
  sizes, 105–106
  words to know, 104–105
concerts, 122
conjugating verbs. *See also*
     verbs
  defined, 20
  irregular, 36–38
  regular, 33–35
consolation phrase, 190
consonants. *See also* vowels
  "b," 11
  "c," 12–13
  clusters, 16
  "d," 11
  double, 15–16
  "f," 12
  "g," 13–14
  "h," 14
  identical pronunciations,
    11–12
  "l," 12
  "m," 12
  "n," 12
  nonexistent, 12
  "p," 12
  pronunciations, 11–16
  "q," 14
  "r," 14–15
  "s," 15
  "t," 12
  "v," 12
  "z," 15
conventions, this book, 2–3
countries
  feminine, 74
  list of, 73–74
  masculine, 74
credit cards, 61, 115
customs. *See also* airports
  agent phrases, 148, 149
  declaration, 149
  words to know, 149

demonstrative pronouns, 173
dessert, 99
dialects, 5
dining. *See also* drinking; eating
  breakfast, 92–93
  dessert, 99
  dinner, 93–98
  lunch, 93–98
  ordering, 97–98
  pasta dishes, 95
  payment, 91
  reservations, 90
  soups, 94–95
  words to know, 98
dinner. *See also* dining; meals
  eating, 93–98
  at home, 94
  out, 94
direct object pronouns. *See also*
     pronouns
  defined, 27
  list of, 27
  use examples, 27–28
directions. *See also*
     transportation
  compass, 156
  distances, 157
  giving/receiving, 159
  giving/receiving verb, 160–161
  giving/receiving vocabulary,
    157–158
  locations, 161–162
  not understanding, 158
  orientation, 156–158
  responses, 156
  spatial relationship terms,
    156–157
  specific place answers,
    155–156
  specific place questions, 155
  verbs for, 159–161
  words to know, 162
distances, 157
doctors
  body parts vocabulary and,
    182, 184
  questions, 182
  talking with, 180–184
  words to know, 184
double consonants
     pronunciation, 15–16

• *D* •

"d" consonant pronunciation, 11
days of the week, 52
decades, 51

drinking. *See also* dining; eating
  drink types, 88
  espresso, 88
  phrases, 87
  quantity specification, 89
  wine, 89
  words to know, 89

• E •

"e" vowel pronunciation, 11
early time, 54
eating. *See also* dining
  breakfast, 92–93
  dessert, 99
  dinner, 93–98
  lunch, 93–98
  meals, 86
  pasta dishes, 95
  phrases, 85
  snacks, 86
  soups, 94–95
  verbs, 95–97
  words to know, 87
e-mail addresses, 55
emergencies
  car trouble, 178–180
  dealing with, 177–188
  doctors and, 180–184
  English-speaking authorities,
    finding, 178
  help, asking for, 177–178
  legal problems, 187–188
  robbery, 185–187
emphasis phrase, 190
English-speaking people
  finding, 67–69
  finding, in emergency, 178
enthusiastic phrase, 189
expressions. *See also* phrases
  favorite, 189–190
  idiomatic, 83–84
  local, 191–193
  popular, 8–10

• F •

"f" consonant pronunciation, 12
fabrics, 107–108
family
  casual conversation, 82
  member names, 81
  talking about, 81–82
  words to know, 82

favorite expressions, 189–190
feelings, expressing, 80
feminine
  body parts, 183
  countries, 74
  nationalities, 75–76
  nouns, 170–171
  ordinal numbers, 49
feminine articles. *See also*
    articles
  definite, 21–22
  indefinite, 23
  plural, 22
food
  baked goods, 113
  famous words, 6–7
  meats, 110
  produce, 111–113
  seafood, 110–111
  shopping, 101, 109–114
  shops, 109–110
  words to know, 113–114
formal greetings, 65
formal introductions, 70
formal pronouns, 30–31
fruits, 111–112
future tense. *See also* tenses
  examples, 42–43
  time marker, 42

• G •

"g" consonant pronunciation,
  13–14
gendered words, 21–25
genderless nationalities, 75
gender-specific nationalities,
  75–76
gifts, bringing, 84
good health phrase, 191
good luck phrase, 191
good-byes
  examples, 63–65
  reuniting and, 66–67
  words to know, 67
grammar
  English/Italian differences, 21
  gendered words, 21–25
  pronouns, 25–31
  questions and, 31–33
  sentences and, 19–21
  tenses, 38–43
  verbs, 20–21, 33–38

greetings
  examples, 63–65
  formal, 64, 65
  informal, 65
  time of day, 64
  words to know, 67

• H •

"h" consonant pronunciation, 14
help
  in accidents, 179
  asking for, 177–178
home. *See also* addresses
  nouns, 56
  verb descriptions, 57–58
homeland conversation
  answers, 73
  countries, 73–74
  informal, initiating, 78
  initiation, 78
  making, 73–80
  questions, 73
  verb/preposition combination,
    76–77
  verbs for, 76–80
hotels
  checking into, 166–169
  plural vocabulary, 171–172
  receptionist, 166
  room reservations, 163–166
  verbs, 166–167
  vocabulary, 169
  words to know, 176

• I •

"i" vowel pronunciation, 11
icons, this book, 3–4
indirect object pronouns
  defined, 28
  list of, 28–29
  use examples, 29
informal greetings, 65, 66
informal introductions, 70
informal pronouns, 30–31
interrogative pronouns
  defined, 31
  list of, 31
  questions using, 32–33
introductions
  examples, 70
  formal, 70, 71

importance, 69
informal, 70, 71
other people, 71–72
pronouns and, 71–72
words to know, 72
yourself, 70–71
investment, 60
invitations, 123
irregular numbers, 48
irregular verbs. *See also* verbs
  conjugating, 36–38
  defined, 33
Italian
  dialects, 5
  English used with, 6
  as romance language, 5
  understanding, 8
Italian words. *See also* words to
    know
  familiar-sounding, 7–8
  famous, 6–7
  gendered, 21–25
  stressing, 16–17

• L •

"l" consonant pronunciation, 12
late time, 54–55
lawyers, 187
legal problems
  explaining, 187–188
  lawyer contact, 187
local phrases, 191–193
lunch. *See also* dining; meals
  eating, 93–98
  time for, 93
  traditional courses, 93–94

• M •

"m" consonant pronunciation, 12
masculine
  body parts, 183
  countries, 74
  nationalities, 75–76
  nouns, 170, 171
  ordinal numbers, 49
masculine articles. *See also*
    articles
  definite, 22
  indefinite, 23
  plural, 22

meals
  breakfast, 86, 92–93
  dessert, 99
  dinner, 86, 93–98
  hotel reservations and, 164
  lunch, 86, 93–98
  payment, 91
meats, 110
mechanics, calling, 179
medical emergencies
  ailment description, 181
  body parts vocabulary,
      182, 184
  doctor, talking with, 180–184
  doctor questions, 182
  phrases, 183
  verbs for, 180–181
  words to know, 184
messages, checking, 142–143
money. *See also* numbers
  bank and, 59–60
  changing, 61
  credit cards, 61
  investment, 60
  words to know, 52, 60–61
months of the year, 51–52
movies. *See also* social events
  going to, 119–121
  questions, common, 120
  subtitles, 120
  words to know, 120–121

• *N* •

"n" consonant pronunciation, 12
nationalities
  country names and, 74
  genderless, 75
  gender-specific, 75–76
nouns. *See also* adjectives;
      pronouns; verbs
  feminine, 170–171
  masculine, 170
numbers
  addresses, 55–58
  cardinal, 45–48
  decades, 51
  irregular, 48
  money, 58–61
  ordinal, 49–50
  phone, 55
  time, 50–55
  times of day, 53

• *O* •

"o" vowel pronunciation, 11
office equipment. *See also* work
  technology-related words, 136
  vocabulary, 137
ordering. *See also* dining
  phrases, 97
  words to know, 98
ordinal numbers. *See also*
      numbers
  defined, 49
  feminine, 49
  list of, 49
  masculine, 49
  use examples, 50
outdoors. *See also* social events
  animals, 126
  nature, 125–126
  phrases, 127

• *P* •

"p" consonant pronunciation, 12
parties. *See also* social events
  invitation verb for, 123–124
  invitations, 123
  words to know, 124
past tense. *See also* tenses
  defined, 38–39
  past participles, 39–41
  structure, 39
pasta dishes, 95
payment
  credit card, 115
  meal, 91
  phrases, 115
  prices and, 115
  shopping purchase, 114–116
  taxi, 152
  verb for, 114–115
  words to know, 116
personal pronouns, 25–26
phone conversations
  answering, 137–138
  asking for people, 141–143
  business/pleasure, 139–141
  cellphones, 138
  chatting, 141
  messages, leaving, 141–143
  phrases, 142
  public phone, 138–139
  saying hello, 137
  verbs for, 139–140
  words to know, 141, 143

phone numbers, 55
phrases
  body parts, 183
  car rental, 150–151
  customs agent, 148, 149
  drinking, 87
  eating, 85
  favorite, 189–190
  hotel check-in, 168
  local, 191–193
  medical emergency, 183
  ordering, 97
  outdoors, 127
  payment, 115
  phone conversations, 142
  public phone calls, 142
  robberies, 185
  slang, 191–193
  time of day, 53
  train ticket purchase, 152–153
  work phone conversation, 142
plurals
  elements, 170
  feminine nouns and, 170–171
  forming, 171
  hotel-related words, 171–172
  masculine nouns and, 170, 171
  nouns ending in *e,* 171
popular expressions
  defined, 8
  list of, 9
  use of, 8, 10
possessive pronouns. *See also*
        pronouns
  agreement, 173–174
  defined, 173
  list of, 174–175
  practical examples, 175
present tense, 42
produce. *See also* food;
        shopping
  fruits, 111–112
  markets, 111
  selecting, 113
  vegetables, 111–112
professions. *See also* work
  list of, 134–135
  talking about, 135
pronouns
  defined, 25, 173
  demonstrative, 173
  direct object, 27–28
  example use, 173

  formal, 30–31
  indirect object, 28–30
  informal, 30–31
  interrogative, 31–32
  introductions and, 71–72
  personal, 25–26
  personalizing, 173–176
  possessive, 173–175
  subject, 25–26
pronunciations
  "a" vowel, 10
  "b" consonant, 11
  "c" consonant, 12–13
  consonant clusters, 16
  "d" consonant, 11
  double consonants, 15–16
  "e" vowel, 11
  "f" consonant, 12
  "g" consonant, 13–14
  "h" consonant, 14
  "i" vowel, 11
  "l" consonant, 12
  "m" consonant, 12
  "n" consonant, 12
  "o" vowel, 11
  "p" consonant, 12
  "q" consonant, 14
  "r" consonant, 14–15
  "s" consonant, 15
  stressing words and, 16–17
  "t" consonant, 12
  this book, 2
  "u" vowel, 11
  "v" consonant, 12
  "z" consonant, 15
public phone calls. *See also*
        phone conversations
  phone cards, 138
  phone numbers, 139
  phrases, 139
public transportation. *See also*
        transportation
  buses, 153–154
  taxis, 151–152
  trains, 152–153
  trams, 153–154
purchases, payment for, 114–116

• Q •

"q" consonant pronunciation, 14
questions
  directions, 155
  doctor, 182

forming, 31
grammar and, 31–33
homeland conversation, 73
hotel check-in, 166
hotel reservation, 164–165
with interrogative pronouns, 32–33
movies, 120
taxi driver, 151
tour booking, 127–128

• *R* •

"r" consonant pronunciation, 14–15
regular verbs. *See also* verbs
  conjugating, 33–35
  defined, 33
rental, car, 149–151
repeat, asking to, 69
replies
  formal greeting, 65
  informal greeting, 66
reservations, hotel. *See also* hotels
  advance, 164
  agent answers, 165
  meal types, 164
  questions, 164–165
  room type, 164
  words to know, 165–166
reuniting, 66–67
robberies. *See also* emergencies
  descriptive vocabulary, 186–187
  phrases, 185
  reporting, 185–186
Romance languages, 5

• *S* •

"s" consonant pronunciation, 15
sales clerk
  clothing words to know, 104–105
  talking with, 104–105
seafood, 110–111
seasons, 50
secret phrase, 191
sentences
  simple, 19–21
  unclear subject, 21

shopping
  baked goods, 113
  clothes, 104–109
  in department stores, 102–104
  departments, 103–104
  food, 101, 109–114
  meats, 110
  prices and, 115
  produce, 111–112
  purchase payment, 114–116
  sales clerk and, 104–105
  seafood, 110–111
  shoes, 109
  sizes and, 105–106
  verb for, 101–102
slang phrases, 191–193
snacks, 86
social events
  concerts, 122
  culture, 117
  information sources, 118
  movies, 119–121
  outdoors, 125–127
  parties, 123–124
  sports, 128–131
  theater seating, 121
  tours, 127–128
  words to know, 119
sports. *See also* social events
  participation, 130–131
  playing, 128–131
  popular, 131
  verbs for, 128–130
streets, 56
stress, word, 16–17
subject pronouns. *See also* pronouns
  defined, 25–26
  list of, 26
  uses, 26
surprise phrase, 189

• *T* •

"t" consonant pronunciation, 12
taxis. *See also* transportation
  destinations, 151–152
  driver question, 151
  hailing, 151
  payment, 152
  time responses, 151

tenses. *See also* verbs
  compound, 39
  future, 42–43
  past, 38–42
  present, 42
theaters, 121
time. *See also* numbers
  days, 52
  decades, 51
  early, 54
  late, 54–55
  months, 51–52
  seasons, 50
time of day
  good-byes and, 64
  greetings and, 64
  speaking versus writing, 53
  words and phrases, 53
tobacco shops, 153
tours. *See also* social events
  booking questions, 127–128
  taking, 127
trains. *See also* transportation
  express, 152
  ticket purchase phrases,
    152–153
trams, 153–154
translations, this book, 2–3
transportation
  airport, 145–149
  buses/trams, 153–154
  car rental, 149–151
  directions and, 154–162
  public, 151–154
  taxis, 151–152
  trains, 152–153
  words to know, 162

• U •

"u" vowel pronunciation, 11
understand, don't, 158

• V •

"v" consonant pronunciation, 12
vegetables, 111–112
verbs. *See also* adjectives;
    conjugating verbs; nouns;
    pronouns
  address, 57–58
  categories, 33

directions, 159–161
eating, 95–97
forms, 20–21
home, 57–58
homeland conversation, 76–80
hotel check-in, 166–167
irregular, 36–38
medical emergency, 180–181
party invitation, 123–124
past participles, 39–41
payment, 114–115
phone conversations, 139–140
regular, 33–35
shopping, 101–102
sports, 128–130
tenses, 38–43
work, 134
vowels. *See also* consonants
  "a," 10
  "e," 11
  "i," 11
  "o," 11
  pronunciation, 10–11
  "u," 11

• W •

weather
  idiomatic expressions, 83–84
  talking about, 82–84
  words, 83
wish/hope phrase, 189
words to know
  airport check-in, 146–147
  breakfast, 92–93
  buses, 154
  car trouble, 180
  clothing, 104–105
  concerts, 122
  customs, 149
  dessert, 99
  dining reservations, 90
  directions, 162
  drinking, 89
  eating, 87
  family, 82
  for financial matters, 60–61, 62
  food shopping, 113–114
  greetings/good-byes, 67
  hotel check-in/settling, 169

hotel reservations, 165–166
hotels, 176
medical emergencies, 184
movies, 120–121
ordering, 98
parties, 124
payment, 116
phone conversations, 141, 143
post-landing, 148
pre-boarding, 147
social events, 119
transportation, 162
work, 136

work
  human element, 135–136
  office equipment, 136–137
  phone conversations, 137–141
  phone phrases, 142
  professions, 134–135
  speaking about, 133–137
  verb for, 134
  words to know, 136

• *Z* •

"z" consonant pronunciation, 15

Notes